Dancing with Whales

Praise for Dancing with Whales

Dancing with Whales: A Book of Encounters is an important book both charming and profound. While each story is lovingly told and each has its own message, taken as a whole, there is a larger message, 'Take care of the world and take care of each other. It's important.' And in addition, it's a pleasurable read. Try it. I think you'll like it.

> —Leland J. Katz, author of *The Pretenders*

Busywork often blocks us from pondering experiences that could take our life-awareness to a deeper level. So Betsy Burr challenges her readers to let our apparently-chance encounters—with people, landscapes, creatures—recharge our awareness and transform our lives.

> —Dr. Virginia Mollenkott,
> Professor Emeritus,
> William Paterson University of New Jersey;
> author of *Sensuous Spirituality: Out from Fundamentalism*

Dancing with Whales changed how I see the world. Each chapter took me on a journey of discovery, opening up unexpected possibilities in everyday events whose significance I might have overlooked in my own life. The result is freeing and refreshing.

> —Mary Olmsted, author of *The Pull of Selves*

Betsy Burr has a mystic's ear and a storyteller's heart. She will inspire you to find these qualities within yourself.

> —Rev. Alison B. Miller, Senior Minister
> Morristown (NJ) Unitarian Fellowship

Fifty-Five Memoir Essays

Dancing with Whales

A Book of Encounters

Betsy Burr

Life is Deep. Come Dive with Me...

DANCING WITH WHALES:
A Book of Encounters

Copyright © 2019 Betsy Burr

ISBN 9781086984330

Photograph of Betsy Burr by Edward Fausty

Cover whale illustration by Dario Fisher | Dario Design | www.dariodesign.co.uk

190802

Dedication

For my wonderfully patient husband,
Stefan, who did daily battle with my
computer for this book,
and my beloved resourceful daughter,
Jessica, whose professional editing skills
helped bring it to life

Contents

Contents

Preface: The Heart of the Matter

H ave you ever wondered how you became yourself?

We become ourselves as we learn about the world: through encountering others. This is the premise of *Dancing with Whales*—fifty-five memoir essays that trace encounters that have shaped me over my lifetime —encounters with people and other creatures and the landscapes we all inhabit, from cougars to cumulonimbus clouds and from an American president to a pauper in a loincloth. This collection also encourages you, the reader, to explore your own life through the same lens.

I am writing here about moments in my life, both positive and negative, that have fortified me and given me insight into leading a more joyful, more meaningful, more interconnected existence.

My fascination with encounters began when I was sixteen. On a beach outing, my schoolmates and I came face-to-face with a pod of California gray whales that rose from the water and onto the sand in front of us. That moment, detailed in the title essay in Section IV, stands out as a metaphor for how my life has progressed.

It's been through such encounters that I experience the world and myself, as I continuously unfold. And so it is for you. To touch another mind with your own is a great adventure—if you bring your whole self with you wherever you go, awake to all life's interconnections, and write or tell stories about it afterwards.

As you read you'll become aware of the transformative power of your own encounters. Think of each essay as a lightning flash in the night, each separate and distinct, each changeful in its own way, and yet all part of the same life story.

At the end of each chapter are a series of suggestions as to how you might relate to my topics with accounts of your own distinctive encounters. Bringing snippets of reality to life can be a lot less intimidating than creating an entire, continuous memoir. If, on reading an essay here, your own stories emerge, beckoning you to share them, jot down a few notes for future reference. As you review your own story, remember to look kindly on your own limitations. A sense of humor about yourself will open your story wide!

Before that day on a California beach, I had only a dim idea of the breadth and depth of human experience. But meeting those whales opened my eyes to wider possibilities. When I looked directly into the eye of the lead whale, I received a silent message which took me years to decipher. As time passed, it affected my relationship to every being I encountered. I eventually learned that "whales," in all their difference and yet similarity to us, their majesty and mystery, are everywhere to be found.

This is the message I came to understand: *The Tree of Life, as it grows, spreads ever more widely, yet each branch and twig is nourished by the same roots. Each life form partakes of this amazing divergence, and this essential oneness. Diversity and Unity are inseparable.* From the time I first understood and lived this truth, I have never felt alone.

Come with me. Discover what you may.

Dancing with Whales

1: Becoming Aware

1: Darkness, Light, Darkness, LIGHT

Long ago, at the beginning of memory, this happened: I am waking up in my crib. A woman comes into the darkened room. She talks cheerfully and goes to the window. She adjusts the blind. Daylight enters and then fades as she lowers it again. For some reason—am I sick?—the always-welcome light is now kept out.

But I don't need it. Inside myself I am being enlightened. In the dimness of the room, I *see*. For the first time, I become aware. It comes to me: this waking-up ceremony has happened before. An old memory-image of someone customarily raising the blind superimposes itself over the present image of the blind now *not* being raised. I see a pattern of choice and change in the contrast—a pattern I can remember and think about. In this moment time has become real for me. It makes me think and see myself thinking. I am becoming myself. Not just actor, but thinker, patterner. Me.

O woman-at-the-beginning-of-memory, the child who now wakes up is not the same child you put down to sleep so short a time ago. All in a moment, as the blind is opened, as the blind is closed, I have begun.

It's your turn now
Further thoughts for readers, writers, and storytellers

What lies at the root of all your recollections? Think back as far as you can go. What did it mean? See if it can be expressed. Is there a jumble of early memories—the taste of your teething ring, your mother's bedtime song, the glow of a candle on your first birthday cake? If you can, write them all down and pursue their meaning for you. They are all parts of your beginning—the building blocks of who you are.

2: Watching the Big People

My first day of nursery school was not a success. Yellowed shades were half-drawn in gloomy, dark-paneled rooms. The large old lady in charge barked out orders. At snack time around a big long table, we were treated to more regulations.

"Now, children, do not talk at the table. And after snack time, fold your napkins and put them in your cubbies. Assemble quickly and quietly in the play room. If you need to go to the bathroom, raise your hand and ask to be excused."

But what was a cubby? I asked the girl next to me to explain. The teacher caught her in the act of responding to my question, scolded her for speaking, and struck her across the face with a flyswatter. Although my childhood self may have exaggerated the memory a bit, the Dickensian image of the flyswatter, black and clotted with the remains of a dead fly, is still vivid in my mind's eye.

I was distressed that my action had led to the girl's punishment, but my strongest feeling was that this adult had done something terribly wrong. When I got home that day, I immediately told my mother. I never went back. I could always count on my mother to be on the side of the Right.

The new nursery school was a big improvement, except for one thing: it had a steep hill leading down to the playground. Every day, children ran pell-mell down that little hill to their favorite swing or slide. Since I was a clumsy child, running often resulted in a fall, a skinned knee, and a trip inside to have my knee cleaned and bandaged. Incidentally, there *were* steps down to the playground, but no other child used them. I would rather skin my knee than be the only one who used the steps.

One day I went for first aid. A pretty young woman greeted me.

"Oh, honey," she said in a sing-song tone. "Have you gone and hurt yourself again? Let's take a look at that. I'll bet it hurts a *lot*." She picked grass from the wound. A young man was hanging out there.

"Aw, kid, you really took a tumble," he said with artificial heartiness. "But we'll have that fixed in no time."

"It's not so bad," I said. "I just don't want to miss recess."

"Now, this is going to sting," the young woman warned me. She applied iodine to the scrape. "But I know you are a brave girl."

"That's right," her companion said. "You are one tough kid."

Although they feigned concern for my small injury, I could see they were really flirting with each other, playing Mommy and Daddy, and using me as a sort of prop for their impromptu romantic scene. I pretended not to notice, but this grown-up interaction, with its artificial ring, fascinated me: people could superficially engage in one activity while really being involved in something completely different.

My mother told me in later years that I had already shown a strong sense of social propriety, at least as I understood it. Once, she said, when she was pushing my stroller—I must have been a little over two—we came upon a man and his son, a boy about my age, standing at the curb. The son had just relieved himself in the gutter, for which his father scolded him. I leaned out of my stroller and vehemently reproached the man.

"Don't scold him for doing that!" I announced. "If he has to go, he has to go!"

My mother told another story from that time. I reproached her friend, saying "*Ladies* don't smoke in the grocery store." And later, outside, "*Ladies* don't smoke on the street, either." Apparently I was judgmental and had to be taught to keep my observations private.

But what I best remember are long hours just watching. I watched my father play ping-pong in the basement with his friends as the ball echoed, *ker-pong, ker-pong*, against the basement walls. I watched my mother feed laundry through the wringer or add the yellow coloring to the pouches of white margarine.

What do all these scraps of memories say about me? Clearly, I was interested in adults. As an only child, with few other children nearby, I interacted primarily with grown-ups. For many years I felt adults were much easier to "decode" than children. No doubt my tendency to behave like a miniature adult did not endear me to other kids!

When I grew up, I understood and enjoyed children. Only then did I strongly appreciate the child in myself. Then, at last, I began to play.

It's your turn now

Further thoughts for readers, writers, and storytellers

What were you like as a small child? You may have to lean on the recollections of the adults who watched you grow. Make what you can of your memories and theirs. What do your earliest memories say about your childhood circumstances, your childhood self? Sights, sounds, smells, feelings—be as specific as you can.

3: Mowing Down Mrs. Moody

P etey Sanford snatched my scooter right out from under my nose and sped across the street. Enraged, my five-year-old self took off after him. Pedaling my tricycle furiously, my ringlets bouncing, I was oblivious to danger.

My short, narrow street was a safe place in Berkeley, California in 1946. Lined with large houses built shoulder to shoulder, with many cars parked curbside, Aspen Avenue was the private world of at least a dozen children who played there daily. Our busy mothers shooed us out the door in the morning and called us home for lunch and dinner.

Unlike the other mothers, mine kept a close watch over her only child. That day, though, she'd gone to the grocery store, leaving two neighbor ladies to watch out for me. But danger can appear everywhere. That day it showed up in the shape of Mrs. Moody.

We lived in the center of the block, right across the street from Mr. and Mrs. Moody, an elderly couple who kept to themselves. Everyone else was compulsively friendly. People said Mr. Moody was a veteran of the Spanish-American War who'd fought with Teddy Roosevelt at the Battle of San Juan Hill—an idea reinforced by his always wearing Rough-Rider-type khaki outfits with Jodhpur pants and riding boots, if not a moustache and pince-nez.

We saw Mr. Moody regularly because he walked to College Avenue every evening to buy his dinner at the Inside Inn and bring it home in a Chinese-food container with a metal handle.

I asked my mother about this odd habit because nobody ate out much in 1946. She told me Mr. Moody didn't trust Mrs. Moody's cooking. Neighborhood gossip had it they always ate separately because he thought Mrs. Moody was trying to poison him—and vice versa.

Their house and ours were the only ones on the block with big side yards. Ours was fenced and had playground equipment. That attracted the neighborhood kids, which my mom liked because she could keep track of us. But when we tired of the swings, rings, and seesaw, we spilled into the street. Sometimes a ball landed in the Moodys' hedged garden. Mr. Moody always refused to let us retrieve it. He called the police, who got the ball for us. On one notable occasion the police retrieved the ball, talked with the Moodys, and presented us with candy bars.

I never dealt directly with Mrs. Moody until six-year-old Petey Sanford stole my scooter. You might say Petey, a blond kid who lived with his mother two doors away, borrowed my scooter. But from my point of view, he snatched it without asking permission—a clear violation of neighborhood etiquette. So I pursued him like one of the Furies, yowling at him.

"Give it baaack!" I cried.

Petey paid me no heed. He sped away across the street, past the Moodys' house. As it happened, lumpy old Mrs. Moody was on the sidewalk trimming a hedge when he dashed past her. Taken by surprise, she turned to find me barreling toward her on my tricycle. She blocked the sidewalk entirely, opened her enormous hedge clippers, and pointed them at my neck.

I screeched to a halt, just in time to avoid hitting Mrs. Moody or having my head chopped off. I can still see those clippers yawning open like the jaws of some prehistoric beast ready to eat me alive. But then an odd thing happened: as we stared at one another in shock, Mrs. Moody fell over backward, stiff as a board, and passed out on the sidewalk, hedge clippers pointed at the sky. They slowly sank into her lap as the two neighbor ladies, aroused by the clamor, came out.

I was outside my mother's charmed circle of protection when they emerged from their houses and saw me, mounted on a tricycle, looming over an unconscious elderly woman. What were they supposed to think? Despite my denials, of course they thought I'd mowed her down.

"She was going to cut my head off!" I wailed.

No one cared. Mrs. Pickett seemed particularly annoyed.

"This has interrupted my radio soap opera at a critical moment," she told Mrs. Hooper.

Never had I felt so alone.

"Call an ambulance!" somebody said.

One came to take away a groggy and protesting Mrs. Moody, minus the hedge clippers. The ambulance people were very reassuring. They said that there was no sign she'd been struck, that she'd probably just been frightened. Still they wanted to run some tests because of her age.

Mrs. Moody passed her tests with what my mother later mysteriously called "flying colors" and was soon home again. Nevertheless, I was an object of suspicion to the neighbor ladies for some time.

At that point in my life, I'd had about five years' experience being a Good Girl. I was good not just because I was praised for it, I think, but because I liked having rules to follow, even though I got teased for it by other kids. Now, however, the tables were turned. I had acquired a Reputation. The neighbor ladies looked at me as a potential troublemaker—I was the girl who mowed down old Mrs. Moody. But to the other kids on the block, for one brief shining moment, I was a celebrity—The Girl Who Mowed Down Old Mrs. Moody.

It's your turn now

Further thoughts for readers, writers, and storytellers

This is the first fleshed-out childhood story that I can recall in detail. As I look back over it, what strikes me most is the feeling of being unfairly treated. According to researchers, children have a strong sense of right and wrong. Can you recall a time in your own childhood when you felt you were wronged? Or think about the first encounter you can remember in detail. Why do you think that story struck you so powerfully? Do you think that one incident reveals something about who you were then?

4: Death or Lunch

I don't know what began The War between the Boys and the Girls when I was nine. Perhaps some combination of lingering resentments and provocations brought things to a head. Someone took Janice's cap pistol and didn't return it; during a ball game the boys didn't play fair with the girls.

No doubt there was name calling, culminating in shoving and little Sally's knee getting skinned. It seemed like the Aspen Avenue boys were ganging up on the girls. What to do?

I took the next step—calling the girls together in a meeting in my basement, which was small and cramped and smelled very earthy. I didn't realize that my life might be at stake in what happened there.

"First off," I declared in my most grown-up manner, "let's size up the problem. The boys are not all that bad. Most are just followers—Scott, Big John, Little John, the Turner brothers, and Eddy, left to themselves, are nice enough. The real problem is Henry Nalex." The brothers Henry and Alex were so inseparable that their two names had melded into one. "They are making the other boys act crazy."

Henry Nalex were wild and unpredictable. Everyone knew about the night they climbed out their second-story bedroom windows ("naked as jaybirds," my mother said) and set out to cross Colby Avenue and cut down the hedge of an older couple they didn't like. They didn't make it. Henry got hit by a car, broke a leg, and was laid up for a while.

"My mother says Henry Nalex are capable of anything," Barbara said glumly. At age ten, she was the oldest, so her words carried extra weight with us all.

"What do we have to fight them with?" asked Karen, who was always practical.

"Let's face it," Barbara said. "We have almost as many people, but no one fierce enough to defeat Henry Nalex." Barbara was probably the most realistic of us.

But Karen wasn't ready to give up.

"We could sneak around and maybe get that cap pistol back, or listen in on their planning meetings."

"If they threw things at us, we could throw things back at them," Sally Hooper, our youngest member, chimed in.

"We may not win, but what if we do nothing?" I asked. "They will just run right over us." It was up to me to rally the troops. "We have to be united. Are we up to the challenge?"

The girls answered with a resounding, "Yes!" We'd been playing on Aspen Avenue with these same boys for five years, and we weren't about to lose our place in the street just because the boys had gotten mean. We agreed we were ready for war. I was chosen as the leader.

After the meeting broke up, I laid out my plans. I got an old recipe tin from my mother, the kind with index cards, and filled out a card for every girl and boy on Aspen Avenue. I carefully listed the strengths and weaknesses of each person—particularly, I am embarrassed to say, noting how well each girl was likely to obey my directions.

We were going to write a letter to the boys declaring war, but right away Karen spilled the beans to her older brother, Big John. Before we knew it the boys had declared war on *us*.

The girls' headquarters was in my basement, and the boys' in Henry Nalex's tree house.

A hiatus followed while everyone figured out what you did when you went to war. I received an anonymous phone call late one evening: "There will be a tennis ball fight in the street on Tuesday at eleven a.m. Be there or else!" A boyish version of a wicked cackle followed.

When the word was circulated, everyone gathered all the old tennis balls they could find. (The neighborhood had a large supply of old, soft tennis balls, which we used in some game we had devised.) We girls took inventory before the fight: we had three tennis balls each.

"The boys might have more," I said, "but when they fire them at us, we will have theirs, so it should all come out even. The main thing is, if you get hit, don't cry, and above all, don't run to your mother."

At 10:55 by my Daisy Duck watch we were all in our places behind parked cars on the girls' side of the street. The boys were ready on their side. At 11:00 the volley began. In the first round, no one hit anybody. A natural lull ensued as kids scrambled to retrieve balls and reconsider strategy.

"Hey, looky—we *did* get some extra balls!" Karen said as she counted them up.

"But what good is that if we can't hit anybody?" fretted Barbara, already discouraged.

I tried to keep spirits up.

"As long as no one hits us, it doesn't matter too much. Let's not throw all our balls in the next round. Next time, hold some in reserve to throw at boys who are out in the open, retrieving balls."

The tactic scored two hits, but the boys also managed to land a couple on the girls.

During the next round, a notable escalation took place as the boys mixed rocks with their tennis balls. The girls did not react well to this. I heard the words "I'm telling Mom" above the fray. When we gathered for our next huddle, we agreed the supply of tennis balls was dwindling as some were landing outside safe reach.

"But we can't throw rocks," Sally cautioned. "People could get hurt and so could the cars." Sally's father drove a laundry truck that didn't belong to him. He had to protect it.

I was still fired up. "If we made a run for the other side of the street, we could capture one of the younger boys at the edge—say, Joey or Mikey Turner—and hold him for ransom. We could get Janice's cap pistol back."

This idea met with limited enthusiasm—groans, actually—but I was ready for anything. I failed to detect just how limited their enthusiasm was.

The next time the boys huddled and Joey Turner wandered off a bit, I said, "Let's go for him!" I ran across the street, only to find not one girl had come with me.

The boys quickly swarmed me. Before I knew it I'd been taken prisoner. As far as the girls were concerned, the war was over. They drifted off, leaving me in the clutches of Henry Nalex.

My hands were quickly tied behind my back. They hustled me over to the boys' headquarters in Henry Nalex's tree house. A Council of War was held to decide what to do next. I was blindfolded with Henry's cowboy kerchief while the discussion progressed, but I knew every boy by his voice.

"Well, what should we do with her now that we've got her?" asked Big John. He was the oldest boy and I'd always kind of liked him. After all, I had hand-fed his snake menagerie when he went to the Boy Scout Jamboree. I couldn't count on him now, though. It was Boys against Girls. There was no changing that.

"We have to make an example of her, so no girl will ever challenge us again," said Eddy. The son of a minister, he was always trying to prove he wasn't a goody-goody.

Henry spoke out decisively: "Let's string her up."

Alex immediately echoed the thought.

"Yeah. Our cousin showed us how to make a hangman's noose, and there's a great rope in Dad's garage."

"That's it, then," Henry said. "Is it the decision of the Council that this girl should be hanged by the neck until dead? All in favor say Aye."

A chorus of Ayes told me my fate was sealed. My heart beat faster. I was sweating. This was beginning to seem real.

In short order someone produced a fairly thick rope and put it over my neck. The knot didn't feel like anything I'd seen in the Boy Scout manual. They hoisted me up on a creaky wooden box, just like we'd all seen on TV. Then they threw the rope over a sturdy branch of the tree-house tree and prepared to carry out their lynching.

I was scared, but it didn't occur to me to scream or struggle. For some reason I just concentrated on playing my part, which, I thought, was to be very brave.

The War Council proclaimed some solemn words over me, justifying my imminent demise, all of which went by in a mindless rush. The scratchy rope tightened around my neck. Suddenly, from across the street came the voice of my mother.

"Betsy! Time for lunch!"

Those words were magic.

"Aw, geez," said Henry, the erstwhile executioner, suddenly a ten-year-old boy once more. The boys grumbled with disappointment, but they weren't up to arguing with a mother's voice.

Reluctantly, they took off my blindfold, untied my hands, and let me go. I got my first peek at the noose around my neck. It looked authentic. I began to think I might really have bitten the dust—or at least had a nasty time of it—if my mother hadn't called me right then. But she *had* called, so I survived.

The War between the Boys and the Girls was over. We girls had lost. My first experience as a leader had ended in defeat when my "followers" abandoned me. After that, I didn't play much on the street. I went to the houses of other playmates from school.

For me, all the fun had gone out of Aspen Avenue.

It's your turn now

Further thoughts for readers, writers, and storytellers

My first attempt at leadership failed disastrously. Looking back, you may have a vivid memory of an incident that put you at risk. Did it mark a change in your life, or your way of thinking? Writing about it may help you understand what happened.

5: An Old Enemy Reappears

C an your worst enemy become your best friend? Over the course of time, I was to find the answer.

Her name was Jean. I called her Mean Jean because she always teased me. She had a reputation for being Bad, and she lived up to it. Not by hitting other girls or smashing things, but by quietly undermining whatever was supposed to happen. Being a Good Girl, I *supported* whatever was supposed to happen. She was slim and blonde. I was dark-haired and a bit chubby. We were polar opposites. Yet fate had drawn us together in the form of a car pool.

In third grade I found myself in a one-room country girl's school. The public school I attended had decided, after the school year began, that I should be bumped up from the second grade, but it had no place to put me. So my parents sent me to a private school in Walnut Creek, almost an hour's drive from our house.

Since Jean lived halfway between my house and the school, our mothers, and another mother of two, decided to share driving duty. I lived the farthest from school, so my mother drove halfway, even on her days off. Sometimes I'd have to wait at Mean Jean's house until my mother picked me up.

Jean snatched whatever book I was reading out from under my nose and ran off with it. She tried to get me to balance plates on my nose and do other tricks I thought were dangerous or Against the Rules. (For the record, Jean balanced plates pretty well and I refused to try.) During naptime at school Jean poked me from the lower bunk bed until I blew up, which got me into trouble.

One of her most irritating qualities was unflinching honesty at awkward moments. Every morning before class, we performed a strange ritual—the Spinning of the Wheel. The names of our various daily duties were printed on a small cardboard wheel—cleaning and shaping our fingernails, polishing our shoes, wearing a bow in our hair, making our beds, and more. The teacher spun an arrow in the middle of the wheel. After we recited the Pledge of Allegiance and sang "God Bless America," the teacher inspected our performance on whatever task the arrow pointed to.

From my point of view, some tasks were more desirable than others. If the fateful arrow landed on Hair Bow, and you weren't wearing one, there was nothing you could do but suffer the disgrace. On the other hand, if the arrow landed on Fingernails, you could at least surreptitiously remedy a lack of cleanliness during "God Bless America."

But best of all was the day the arrow landed on Making My Bed because no one could verify whether you'd made your bed that morning. As a result, every girl reported having made her own bed—until it came to Jean, Mean Jean, who said in her haughtiest tone of voice, "My *maid* makes my bed."

With that simple five-word sentence, Jean managed to alienate every single person in the room—the girls who made their own beds, the girls who lied about making their own beds (including me), and certainly the teachers, who were probably paid less than Jean's nanny.

I was profoundly shocked she would flaunt her nanny at us all, and just as shockingly, not even give lip service to the notion she should make her own bed. But a small part of me—the part that didn't make my bed and lied about it—admired Mean Jean's courage when she told the truth, whatever the consequences.

Jean disappeared from my life after that one year, but she always stood out in my mind as the quintessential enemy of my early childhood school years.

Fast forward six years to the beginning of my freshman year at the Anna Head School in Berkeley. As I looked through papers explaining our first class get-together, I made a horrifying discovery: Mean Jean was to be one of my forty classmates. I'd already been at the school for one year. I'd had a difficult time adjusting at first, but by June had found friends and a much-wanted place on the school newspaper. I'd been looking forward to a good year.

I complained bitterly to my mother.

"She will make school miserable for me, just the way she did in the third grade!" I wailed.

But my mother was a warm and wise woman. What she said next changed my life.

"It doesn't have to be like that, Betsy. Jean is not a bad person. In fact, I can imagine the two of you becoming friends. Remember, Jean doesn't know anyone at your school. You have the advantage of knowing the teachers and the students and knowing your way around. You could be a big help to her—if you choose to be. I suggest that when you meet her in that reception line tomorrow, you remind her who you are and give her a big welcome, just as if you were old friends. I bet she'll be grateful. This could be the start of something good for you, too. Why not give it a try?"

The next day I followed my mother's suggestion and in the reception line greeted Jean warmly. I got just the response my mother had anticipated. Jean and I became fast friends—best friends throughout high school.

Jean's friendship was important for me. She taught me to loosen up—a much-needed lesson after my Good Girl start in life. When I slept over at her house, we would sneak out the second-story bedroom window, climb down the trellis so redolent of sweet-smelling star jasmine blossoms, and go into the pool house. There we played billiards until the wee hours, listening to music our parents wouldn't approve of.

As exam times loomed, Jean suggested we adopt a foreign accent, different every term, which we adhered to religiously throughout finals week. What a terrific technique for relieving the stress of exams! Jean was a wonderful mimic, picking up accents with speed and accuracy. All I had to do was imitate her. Since we always got good grades, our parents bemusedly put up with our antics.

Mean Jean blossomed into a lovely girl and wonderful woman—brilliant, funny, and supremely generous of spirit. She was a treasured friend until her death from cancer at age forty-eight.

Were it not for my mother preparing me for our encounter at age thirteen, I never would have had those years of pleasure in her company.

It's your turn now

Further thoughts for readers, writers, and storytellers

Your longest friendship—isn't it a treasure that grows richer with time? Don't take your memories of it for granted. Compare notes with your friend. You may be surprised to find how you remember different incidents or remember the same ones differently. Forgive all, celebrate all, and write it down! And don't overlook the small details—like the fragrant star jasmine that grew on the trellis we climbed down at night. These small touches make a story come alive!

6: High Sierra Thunderstorm

We were up above timberline, riding our horses across a great granite dome, when a thunderstorm broke over us—my mother, my father, and ten-year-old me. It was my first pack trip, but my parents were experienced trail-hands in these California mountains. Midsummer thunderstorms were rare in the High Sierras, but when they came, even I knew you didn't want to be the tallest thing around. On the crest of this enormous rock formation, we were set up for a lightning strike.

We quickly dismounted.

"At least the horses will be taller than we are," my mother joked.

But of course, if the horses were struck, we'd probably be just as dead.

My mother rummaged through the saddlebags for the latest thing in raingear. I put on my crackling new plastic poncho, but before it could settle into place, high winds and an assaulting rain tore it off my body. My mother and father soon suffered the same fate. Five minutes into the storm, we were exposed to the elements and drenched through, as lightning cracked open the skies.

Our horses whinnied nervously, shivered, and stamped their feet. Fortunately, despite the crashes of thunder and lightning around us, they and our single pack mule stood their ground.

My father shouted instructions over the relentless roar of the wind.

"The storm is blowing at our backs, which is good," he said, "but there's no shortcut. We'll just keep walking toward our base camp."

After a mile, we took shelter under an overhanging rock ledge and stayed there until the storm passed. The ledge was narrow, rough, and damp. It would not have protected us from lightning, but we were grateful for the illusion of refuge.

After the storm moved on, we remounted our patient horses and rode another few miles to our destination in a valley beside a small stream. We set up camp in the advancing twilight. We had no tent—just an oilcloth that protected our sleeping bags from the wet ground. The horses and the mule were hobbled, and we set them out to feed in the adjoining meadow.

We gathered damp wood. Using a lighter and newspapers from home, my father managed to start a fire for supper. Mother heated canned stew and we ate packer's bread, fresh from the bakery that morning. We went to sleep under a gloriously starry sky. I'd made it through my first day of a pack trip in the High Sierras. I was damp, cold, saddle-sore, and supremely happy. Our brush with death brought home to me the beauty of life and the glory of the wilderness. I nodded off, happy to belong to this adventurous little family.

Two days later a ranger rode up to our base camp, a train of horses strung out behind him. He stopped for a cup of coffee with my parents. The adults shooed me off, but I lingered nearby to overhear their conversation.

"What are those duffel sacks laid over the backs of your pack horses?" my father asked the ranger.

"Dead bodies, one to each horse—the corpses of six people who took refuge during the storm under a large tree in the valley just beyond this one. When lightning hit the tree, they were electrocuted. The coins in their pockets are all fused together."

While he talked, I sidled over to the lead horse and stroked him gingerly, mindful of the burden he bore on his back. I had never been so close to the great mystery of death. If a bolt of lightning had veered this way instead of that, my parents and I would have occupied those body bags. But it had not.

We were alive. They were dead. That was the only part I could comprehend.

It's your turn now

Further thoughts for readers, writers, and storytellers

When and where did you first encounter death, not theoretically but in solid reality? How did it affect you? Putting pen to paper may help you get perspective on it. If you do, start your story out with a bang and build the tension.

II: Connecting

7: Two Esthers, Lazarus, and Me

A few years ago I came across a copy of *Lazarus Laughed*, Eugene O'Neill's play about the friend of Jesus whom he resurrected from the dead. A hazy fifty-year-old memory surfaced of a University of California (Berkeley) production in which my ten-year-old self had been a chorus member. Intrigued, I opened the library copy to act one, scene one, and read the chorus's opening lines: "He that believeth shall never die! Lazarus, come forth!" With a shock of recognition, a door suddenly opened into 1951, the year I was in the play—the year my Aunt Esther died.

Back then I was the only child in a household of four adults whose average age was sixty-two. In addition to my parents, they were Mother B., my father's mother, whose quiet presence dominated our house, and her younger sister, my Great-Aunt Esther. In the smoldering guerrilla war between my mother and her mother-in-law, I sided with my mother, but my best friend and ally was Aunt Esther. Like me, she was an onlooker. Finally, my mother took a job—to get away from the two old ladies, she said—so sometimes, when my grandmother was away visiting her daughter, Aunt Esther and I were the only ones around. We became close after a particular incident.

One day when I was six, I got into trouble over a dime missing from the kitchen table. I protested that I hadn't taken it. When the adults found a dime in my pocket, I said I'd found it on the sidewalk, but they met this alibi with some skepticism. In those days, a dime was a significant amount of money. It could buy a single-scoop cone at Bott's ice cream store. But there was a lesson about trust to be learned.

Aunt Esther made me a bargain.

"I'll tell you what," she said. "I'm going to leave some change in a silver dish on my dresser. If you ever need some money, just come and take what you need. It will always be there for you." And it always was.

I only took money from the covered dish once—a single dime. I knew Aunt Esther was on welfare and had to live very frugally. The dish became a symbol of her unfailing support. I knew I could count on her sympathetic ear and warm, soft hugs.

Fast forward four years to the fall of 1951, when I got the chance to be a member of the Greek chorus of *Lazarus Laughed*. I didn't consider myself to be a Christian, but I loved the Biblical mystery stories as I did the Greek myths. The play was staged outdoors in a stone replica of a twenty-five-hundred-year-old Greek theater. Rubbing elbows with college-age actors and actresses, who were both grown-up and young and vital, excited me. I had a huge crush on the black-haired, black-eyed actor who played Lazarus.

At the dress rehearsal, I inhaled the enticing aroma of greasepaint and saw the Greek masks gleaming in the light of our torches. They enchanted me. I felt an eerie sense of actually participating in a miracle story almost two thousand years old.

When I got home I learned Aunt Esther had died of a heart attack. After dinner she had taken her usual stroll to the local pharmacy, where she loved chatting with the druggist and his wife in the quiet of evening. Crossing the street to the drugstore, she was suddenly stricken. Someone told me she died "before she hit the pavement."

I was thunderstruck. I felt guilty I had been out. Worse than that, I'd been transported into another world when I should have been at home. *Maybe then she wouldn't have died*, I thought. *This is something I need to talk to Aunt Esther about.* Then came the realization: that conversation would never take place. Aunt Esther was really gone.

Opening night arrived. As I waited backstage with the chorus of Lazarus's neighbors, my feelings were a jumble of apprehension, sadness, and guilt. Unable to concentrate, I needed to talk. I found a ready listener in my stage mother, a college student also named Esther. I told her about the money dish.

"That was very special," the young Esther told me. "I'll bet you will always remember that dish when you think of Aunt Esther." She shared some special memories of her grandmother, who also had died recently.

Though I had no words for it then, a feeling of connectedness eased my grief.

At last the play began. We chorus members lined up, each carrying a torch waiting to be lit—the illumination for this outdoor evening production. One by one, each torch was set ablaze. One by one, we made our entrances. I can almost hear our chant as we questioned the risen Lazarus: "Is there hope of love for us on Earth? Why are we bound to die? ... What is beyond, Lazarus?"

And then echoed his exultant answer: "Life! Eternity! Stars and dust! God's eternal laughter!"

By the flickering torchlight came the chorus's response: "Laugh! Laugh! We are stars! We are dust! There is only God! We are his laughter!" A weight lifted off me, as joy descended through the night sky.

My stage mother was right. I have never forgotten Aunt Esther, or the trust and love represented by that money dish. Later, when I became a mother, I put the silver dish on my dresser and explained to my daughter that if she ever needed a little extra money, it was there for her. There are no children in my home now, but Aunt Esther's money dish is still on my dresser, carrying its living message to the child that's in me still.

It's your turn now

Further thoughts for readers, writers, and storytellers

Do you remember, as a child, suffering a great loss? Feeling guilty about something beyond your control? What happened to comfort you? If you were not reassured or comforted, what were the consequences? How has this loss echoed through your life?

8: Challenged to Think

Teenagers live in another country from the one they've traversed since infancy. Sometimes they need a fresh set of guides through this new terrain—guides with ways of thinking and acting so powerful they can shape one's mind and future. Good fortune gave me Daniel and Catherine Dewey.

The Deweys were headmaster and headmistress of the Anna Head School in Berkeley, California, where I spent eighth grade through senior high. I knew them primarily through what they taught—in Mrs. Dewey's case, as the advisor to the school newspaper. She was known as a dragon lady, or more politely as a defender of high standards. I joined the paper as an uncertain thirteen-year-old freshman taken with the romance of the fourth estate. (Our little monthly paper was put together on the great linotype machines of *The Berkeley Daily Gazette*, our town newspaper. We spent a lot of time with the old-time printers and linotype operators in their magical realm.)

My first crisis arose while meeting tight deadlines—not my work, but my responsibility. I was petrified, sure I'd lose my privileged position. The fearsome Mrs. Dewey came by, looked over the situation, and very cheerfully said, "Don't panic!" She led us through the disaster.

I always remembered "Don't panic!" as some of the best advice I ever received. She delivered it often to one or another of us. She taught me how to organize, stay on schedule, and deliver the goods under pressure. Thanks to her leadership, the paper won a statewide award—the year after I left.

Encountering Daniel Dewey—our headmaster, who was to teach us Ancient History—was for me like coming up against a great force of nature. He'd been a classical archaeologist, so he really knew whereof he taught. Moreover, he resembled an ancient Roman senator like the ones in our textbooks—chiseled in marble, stern-faced, handsome. He was the model of the ethical man, but he always had a smile playing around his lips. We knew he'd meet our imperfections with a sense of humor.

On the first day of class he scanned the room and made an announcement: "As lowly freshmen, you are no doubt very ignorant." He said this with a relish that made the condition seem almost tolerable. "I am determined that you will come away from this course with some sense of the wisdom of the ancients. By your presence here, I assume you are ready for that. Is it so?"

"Yes," we chorused in some bewilderment.

"Very well, then, let us begin."

We soon got our first glimpse of "the wisdom of the ancients." He had us read the first two paragraphs of our textbook on the history of ancient Greece. We came to the phrase "Crete turns her face to the islands [of the Aegean Sea] and her back to Egypt." Mr. Dewey stopped us dead in our tracks.

"So, is that clear to you?"

We all nodded yes, hoping to stay out of trouble.

"Then what does it mean?"

Not one of us had the foggiest idea. We waited expectantly for him to tell us, but that was not to be. He explained what a metaphor was and how important they were in ancient Greek culture.

"What metaphor is being used in this sentence?" he asked.

"A woman's body is being used as a metaphor for the island of Crete, with a face on one side and a back on the other," I said. I believed in speaking up early in the semester, assuming I knew anything at all. Then I could relax for a while.

"Good," Mr. Dewey said. "But why? What does it mean?"

I was not off the hook. I couldn't answer the question.

For the next hour, Mr. Dewey went into his Socratic questioning mode, about which we would learn more later, trying to pry answers from our fuzzy little minds.

"What is the role of the face, as opposed to the back?" he asked Jennifer.

"It's to look at," she answered, confidently.

"Ah, but why do we look at faces?" countered Mr. Dewey.

"Because your face is who you are," said a pretty girl.

This was not the answer Mr. Dewey was looking for. His level of impatience rose visibly as he paced the front of the room.

"'Your face is who you are,'" he echoed. "Does anyone want to comment on that?"

His ironic tone was not lost on us.

"Looks aren't everything," I responded. I was embarrassed and self-conscious about my acne, but I forced the words out. "The face also speaks, and that's important."

"Excellent!"

I breathed a gigantic sigh of relief to hear Mr. Dewey direct this word at me.

"What other jobs does the face do?" he asked.

Eventually, he got us to the point of saying, "The face takes in food, air, and vision and sends out words and emotions." He pressed on with his Socratic method, sometimes thundering his questions at us. But by the end of the session, to his obvious relief, we got the idea that on islands things come and go through harbors—it took us a long time to think of harbors—so the harbors must face the Aegean Sea, with perhaps spine-like mountains to the south, on the Egypt side.

We never progressed beyond that one sentence that day, but I left the room exhilarated. I'd entered a new world of thinking: if I ask myself the right questions, my mind could figure things out for itself. Sixty-three years later, I still treasure my copy of *History of Ancient Greece* and what I learned in its first chapter.

Later, when we turned our attention to Rome, Mr. Dewey had us read a book on ancient Roman kings, good and bad, starting with Romulus, who founded Rome in 756 BC, and his successors. The lesson culminated with the reign of Tarquin the Proud, who killed the previous king and his own wife and was in turn overthrown, leading to the establishment of the Roman Republic in 509 BC.

We were tested on our reading of the book. When our tests had been graded and returned, Mr. Dewey paused. He looked around the room, long and hard.

"That's all well and good, but none of it ever happened," he said. "The kings of ancient Rome are mythological."

We all sat dumbfounded.

"Why would you have us read a book about things that never happened?" I asked.

"Because the ancient Romans *believed* the kings of ancient Rome were real, and their beliefs influenced Roman history. For example, a Brutus supposedly killed Tarquin the Proud and ushered in the Roman Republic, so Romans who wanted to bring back the Republic when Julius Caesar was emperor felt a Brutus should be the one to kill Caesar. History was very important to the Romans."

"But how come a modern author would write a book as if the kings of Rome were real?" I asked.

"Look at the date in the front of your book and you will see it was published some years ago," Mr. Dewey said. "Since then, modern scholars have agreed the kings of Rome were creations of later Romans to explain a history for which they had no record. I hope you will learn from this not to believe everything you see in print."

My mind buzzed as I went away from that class. If I wasn't to believe everything I saw in print, maybe I shouldn't believe everything I heard in class, either. What if "modern scholars" of the next generation decided at least some of the ancient kings of Rome were real? Perhaps that's just the lesson Mr. Dewey would most have wanted me to learn.

By the way, the last time I checked the *Encyclopedia Britannica* on-line, it said Tarquin the Proud is accepted by some scholars today as an actual historical figure.

In my junior year Mr. Dewey set aside one hour a week, on Wednesday afternoons, when he and I could talk. He was interested in what I thought about everything, from the second Stevenson/Eisenhower presidential race to the founding of Ghana, the first nation in sub-Saharan Africa to gain independence. I was eager to talk about any topic Mr. Dewey brought up on our long walks around the school grounds. Mostly, he fended off my questions about his opinions. I was definitely the student. His questions always led me deeper into every subject than I'd ventured on my own.

Toward the end of that year, he told me he'd be teaching American History to the senior class—my class, of course.

"I really don't know very much about American history," he said, off-handedly. "I wonder which one of us will know more about American history by next fall—you or me?"

I came to, abruptly, as if I'd been tapped in the solar plexus. What? Me learn more than the teacher between spring and fall? But I knew a challenge when I heard one. I was up for it.

Immediately my mind whirled with calculations about my strengths and weaknesses in American history. My only real strong point was the Civil War era: a love of Abraham Lincoln had drawn me into reading rather widely on my own. My family planned a three-week trip to the East Coast that summer, which would inevitably involve visiting many historical sites, particularly those connected with the colonial era and the Revolutionary War. I concentrated my efforts on everything before Reconstruction, figuring Mr. Dewey would be forced to cover all American history. If everything went well, I might just have an edge for the first few months.

Of course, there was no such thing as having an edge over an experienced teacher like Mr. Dewey, but we had many dynamic classroom conversations about the great issues of early American history. He was a wonderful sparring partner. That course was one of the great delights of my life. And of course, just as Mr. Dewey had planned, I learned a great deal about independent study.

The puzzles Mr. Dewey regularly set before us and the hoops he made us jump through gave me confidence in myself—a confidence that had been lacking. For this I will be everlastingly grateful.

As the year passed, though, I sensed a hardening in Mr. Dewey's manner. He was less patience with classroom foibles. We always knew he loved us. That knowledge remained unshaken. But one day, frustrated that we couldn't grasp his point, he broke his chalk pointer over one classmate's desk. I think the action shook him as much as it shook us. We were used to Jove thundering but not to his starting a brush fire so close to home. The lines in Mr. Dewey's face grew a little sterner. The twinkle in his eye was less easy to come by.

We didn't know then that the University of California had announced its intent to convert our building into a university facility and boot us out. Mr. and Mrs. Dewey owned the school, so he had a lot on his mind. Where would they take it? Where *could* they take it? Berkeley was overdeveloped as it was.

Eventually, the Deweys found a new home for the school in Oakland, but we had graduated by then. I never fully identified with the new place. Before very long, the Deweys sold the school. My deepest tie with it was broken.

In their retirement years, I was married, raising a young daughter and working for the New Jersey State Senate as a legislative analyst. I had lost touch with the Deweys. One day a bulletin from the school arrived telling of both their deaths.

As I absorbed the devastating facts, my mind leapt to a bright spring day when I'd rounded up the Deweys and Freckles, Mrs. Dewey's small terrier mutt companion, for their 1958 yearbook picture. That very photo, with Freckles curled at their feet, was in the bulletin.

Mrs. Dewey, it said, had died after a long struggle with cancer. Mr. Dewey had nursed her through it and died soon afterwards. The notice referred to their four daughters, who survived them. One lived in Morris-town, New Jersey, where I lived. I immediately tried to track her down, only to discover she actually lived in Moorestown, in a distant part of the state.

On second thought, I realized, the bulletin was not so far off. The Deweys *did* have a daughter living in Morristown, New Jersey.

It's your turn now

Further thoughts for readers, writers, and storytellers

Remember the greatest teachers you ever had? By sharing stories of them, you can honor their memory and pass it on.

9: Stefan Appears

Our relationship began with a lie.

In my senior year of high school, a mutual friend told me she knew a boy who wanted to go to the Senior Prom of our girls' school.

"He'd be a great date for you," she said.

I was deep in my studies, having sworn off boys after a failed two-year relationship. I declined.

"Oh, come on," she pleaded, laughingly. "You study too hard. 'All work and no play,' you know the saying."

"Nope. I've done very well this last year without a boy to take up my thoughts, and I think I'll just keep it that way for now."

"Stefan is a freshman at Berkeley. I've known his family forever. He is very bright, so he can keep up with you. And he has an amazing mother. You'll love her."

Pat was also very bright. She was warm, insightful, and a good soul. After a bit more wheedling, I reluctantly came around, partly because the "amazing mother" intrigued me.

Little did I know that Pat then went to the boy in question and told *him* she knew a girl who wanted to go to the prom. She told him we would make great partners.

"She is very bright," Pat said, "so she can keep up with you."

"But I don't like to dance," he protested. "I wouldn't know a waltz from a two-step. Besides, I'm very busy with my studies."

"Oh, come on," she said, echoing her strategy with me. "She's an amazing person, and you can't just study all the time."

"But it would feel awkward to just go to a dance with someone I don't know."

"Then meet her for coffee at a cafe near the University. Her school is nearby. You can do this."

"I don't drink coffee," he said, "but I suppose I could have a soft drink."

Before we two reluctant teens knew it, we were face to face.

I saw before me a tall, gangly seventeen-year-old with crew-cut sandy hair, dressed in an ROTC uniform, which suited him very well. (This was before the Vietnam Era, and all freshmen men were enlisted in the Reserve Officers' Training Corps.) I, with my short, dark hair and somewhat earnest expression, wore my high school uniform—a gray sweater and skirt with a tidy white blouse—and hoped I looked presentable.

Though awkward and out of practice, we searched for something in common and hit upon science fiction and folk music.

"Maybe we could get tickets to the folk concert at the University this weekend," he offered.

I guessed that might be fun.

The concert went well enough. I thought this dance business might be okay after all. But then his "amazing" mother refused to let him go to the all-night party afterward. She felt it was too long and dangerous a drive home for a relatively inexperienced driver who hadn't slept. I was furious! I would miss half the fun of the date! (It turned out later that she was right. The ride home again *was* long and dangerous, and one car filled with prom-goers was to have a serious accident. Fortunately, no lives were lost.)

When prom night arrived, as we drove through the rainy darkness to the pre-prom dinner, I had an odd thought. *This stormy and pitch-black drive with this boy/man will be repeated over and over through a lifetime.* The reflection startled me because I had ambivalent feelings toward my date. Nevertheless, the thought left a strong impression.

The dance proved to be a disappointment. He really didn't know how to dance, and kept asking, "Is this a waltz or a two-step?" The long, tedious evening fulfilled my misgivings. At last the dance ended. On the drive home I made a vow: this guy was not, repeat *not*, going to get to kiss me. Imagine the nerve of him. He wanted a date for the prom but didn't know how to dance!

At my front door I prepared to turn away any approach he might make. But, to my rage, he didn't even try to kiss me. That was the last straw!

A week went by. I cooled off. When he finally called, he asked if I'd go to a lecture at the University. Intrigued by the topic, I agreed.

So began a friendship, which after two years somehow mutated into something more. Almost five years after that prom night, on the day with the longest night of the year, we married in the little redwood chapel in Yosemite Valley, a day of deep happiness and fulfilment.

Ten years later we finally discussed that uncomfortable prom and discovered Pat had conned us both. In the fifty-five years since, we've had many happy times, but we've never, but ever, gone to another dance.

It's your turn now

Further thoughts for readers, writers, and storytellers

Meeting a new person can be fraught with possibilities, both positive and negative. Call to mind an experience of your own that began badly and blossomed into something more. Be as specific as you can!

10: Two Transformations

"The cord is wrapped around the baby's neck," the doctor said. "It's cutting off breathing with every contraction."

I'd been given an epidural anesthetic. Until that moment I thought the first six hours of my first delivery had gone well.

"You're going to need to get this baby out as fast as possible," he continued. "Push as hard as you can."

I followed his instructions, but inside I was stricken. My parents had lost two babies carried full term—stillborn for different reasons. *Now it's my turn to lose a child*, I thought. *I always knew this might happen.* I felt the terrible loss of anticipated joy.

But physically, I was trying. I pushed determinedly. After a long interval, the baby emerged.

"It's a girl," the doctor reported. He held her up. She was limp and blue. My worst fears were being confirmed. The doctor took her aside to suction mucus from her mouth and vigorously slap her back. After what seemed an age, his efforts worked. The baby jerked to life, emitting a healthy cry.

Doctor, nurses, and I all breathed a sigh of relief and rejoiced in this turn of events. Then they placed the baby in my arms.

"A girl," I echoed, amazed. I had always wanted a daughter but had convinced myself to be equally happy if I had a boy. I was holding the girl of my dreams. My grief turned to rapture. Her birth felt like a miraculous resurrection.

As I gazed into her small red face, she gazed directly into my eyes with a piercing intensity that took me completely by surprise. After living in the dark, when she came into the light, how did she know where to look? This mysterious instinctive response overwhelmed me. I softly cried, echoing her whimpers. She was here, her own person, yet our actions mirrored one another. A strong, enduring bond was formed.

Once a waiting fetus, she was now a newborn girl. I had been a woman prepared for sorrow. Now I was a mother pledging my life to hers.

It's your turn now

Further thoughts for readers, writers, and storytellers

Of all the encounters in your life, is there one that evokes the deepest emotions—perhaps a lover, perhaps a child? Only you can tell that tale.

11: Moons with a Message

My husband finally got me to the local astronomical society around 1972. It was their night for telescope viewing and a chance to see something new.

I was not particularly interested in telescopes and the information—highly mathematical, it seemed to me—enthusiasts derived from using them. I imagined we'd see a scattering of circular objects, some pinpoint-sized, painted on the dome of heaven. Though I'm visually oriented, I am more at home with art than science.

That night the sky was moonless. Streetlights weren't as ubiquitous back then, so prospects for viewing were good. A couple of telescopes were mounted in the parking lot of a local museum. We saw various stars and planets, which stirred mild interest in me. As I'd expected, they were dots and circles of light. I uttered the appropriate sounds of pleasure, but frankly, I wasn't engaged.

Suddenly, everything changed: we were shown an image of Jupiter and its moons. To my complete surprise, I was overcome with wonder. What did I see that so amazed me? I saw order and regularity in what had always seemed to me to be a chaotic night sky.

For thousands of years humanity has tried making sense of the heavens. The ancient Greeks and Chinese traced the outlines of mythical heroes and astrological animal life by connecting star to star. Other civilizations detected a clock-like repetition in the movements of the sun on the horizon, as Stonehenge and the Mayan temples in Mexico attest.

All very well and good, but before me was something even more striking—a single snapshot of Jupiter flanked by four visible moons, strung out like beads on a taut fish-line. The image clearly pointed to order in the scheme of things. A natural regularity governed celestial bodies, hinting at much more.

Of course I knew Newton's laws were at work. But dim familiarity with those precepts hadn't prepared me for seeing such a linear formation. It was like seeing a miniature vision of the solar system.

Think about it. Where do we see order, as our human minds visualize it, in nature? The physical world, to the naked untutored eye, usually appears as random and irrational as clouds in the sky or blades of grass on a lawn. Throughout human history, and even further back in time, we've searched through chaotic reality for recognizable patterning.

The moons of Jupiter are exceptions to the apparent randomness in the star-strewn sky. All that's needed is a simple low-powered telescope, an absence of streetlights, and a cloudless, moon-free night, and I had seen it, too—one of nature's essential patterns. It was like a message from the universe, directed at me personally, if only I could read it—a Morse code message, written among the stars.

It's your turn now

Further thoughts for readers, writers, and storytellers

You don't have to be a scientist to experience the excitement that scientific explorations can inspire. Consider a time when you were awed by what was revealed.

12: One Deep Breath

Have you ever experienced a moment that changed how you saw, not just some things, but everything?

In the spring of 1980, I was president of my congregation, the Morristown (NJ) Unitarian Fellowship. Our church had spent two years without a minister as we searched for a new one. When the Search Committee, of which I was a member, found a promising candidate, we invited him and his family to visit us for one week.

When he arrived he delivered the Sunday sermon, visited with many committees and groups, and spoke again on the final Sunday morning. Then he left the congregation to its deliberations.

Discussion was brisk, as Unitarians love working things through. The future of our Fellowship was at stake. Finally, it was voting time. As I conducted the meeting, it fell to me to lead the oral tally. Everyone looked at me expectantly. Would it be thumbs up or thumbs down? Even a few negative votes probably meant the candidate would turn us down.

I took a deep breath and called for the vote, and something entirely unexpected happened: the breath I took in was meaningful in ways I cannot describe, except by analogy. Imagine experiencing your life in two dimensions and it suddenly turns to three. Or imagine your life in black-and-white turning suddenly to color. Everyday meanings all around me, meanings ignored in the customary course of events, suddenly became evident. The history of our congregation and the complexity of every person I faced seemed to be unveiled simultaneously.

I paused to take it all in. The congregation must have thought I paused for effect. They waited patiently. In another moment, I led the vote count. A minute later it was over. I announced the unanimous approval of our new minister, and a new chapter in our congregational life began.

I felt a great elation, not only because we had accomplished our mission but because a deep sensation of wholeness continued past the meeting and over time. It changed how I experienced my life.

Some might say I had sensed a "calling." I felt that myself. But I didn't interpret it as a call to enter the ministry—family circumstances didn't allow that option—but rather a call to live with greater awareness of my fellow creatures and our interdependence in the web of existence.

Wait a minute, my friends might say, you're an agnostic—you believe that existence is too profound to comprehend. Yes, it's true. Like many agnostics, I'm content to pursue what I *can* know and live comfortably with the ultimately incomprehensible.

I do believe, although I can't define it, that there's a matrix which holds me and binds me together with all the rest of existence. I delight in exploring the ways existence is interconnected, but beyond that, I let the mystery be.

Then who, or what, called me? I don't know, but I imagine a deep part of me opened to receive a profound truth that's always waiting to be found—a truth about the nature of reality: There is a Oneness of which I am a part. Somehow I've managed to hold onto the vision. I do this by hunkering down, suppressing my ego and its demands—"I want!" "I need!"—so I can more clearly respond to this wholeness in its many manifestations.

Do I manage to do this all the time? No. Sometimes, after all, I have to listen to my own needs and wants. And often I just fail, missing messages that Walt Whitman called "letters from God," which he found in the most ordinary places. (Even as an agnostic, I use religious wording such as "God" and "calling" when they metaphorically convey a psychological truth.)

As an agnostic, I take all pronouncements with a grain of salt, including my own. Yet this I know: life has been more abundant for me since I took that one deep breath.

It's your turn now

Further thoughts for readers, writers, and storytellers

Have you ever experienced a spiritual encounter that moved you to the core? It might have been during a walk in nature, or in a deep connection with another person or creature, or in some other way. If you have not, how do you find your way to it? By staying open to meaning, wherever it is found. Such events, once experienced, are often very hard to write about, but you may find the effort very rewarding.

III: Watching Creatures Close to Home

13: The Shadrach Wars

When the day arrived for my first horseback ride, I catapulted out of bed and eagerly performed my morning rituals. I donned my fresh-pressed dress, polished my saddle shoes, made my bed, and affixed a bow to my well-brushed hair—all part of the requirements at the private, one-room country schoolhouse where I'd just started third grade, in late fall. The best part was packing up the T-shirt, corduroy pants, and Keds I'd need for my great afternoon adventure.

All morning Mrs. Stone taught, but I could hardly pay attention. As she talked about the Pilgrims' Thanksgiving story, I dreamed of the noble, prancing steed that awaited the touch of my knowing hand on his reins.

Reality proved somewhat different. As the stable enfolded me in the intriguing odors of hay and manure, I waited impatiently as all the other girls mounted their customary horses. I was directed to the last remaining horse, Shadrach, a swaybacked old gelding with a distinctly scruffy white coat. He regarded me balefully out of his one good eye.

"We're so glad to have you join us," said the instructor, "even though you are starting late. Have you ever ridden before?"

"Oh, yes," I breathed earnestly, recalling frequent rides on the local merry-go-round.

"That's good, because we are going out on a trail ride today. If you hadn't ridden before, you would have to stay back at the stables and ride around the ring. Do you feel comfortable riding on the trail?"

"Oh, yes!" I said, full of confidence in all I had learned from reading *Black Beauty*.

She helped me into the Western-style saddle as the other girls watched from atop their sleeker mounts.

Off we went into the grassy hill country of northern California. More accurately, off the others went. Shadrach apparently had decided his new rider was not worthy of him. No matter how earnestly I kicked his sides and shook the reins, as the instructor urged me to do, he refused to budge.

"Don't worry," the instructor said. "Shadrach just needs a little encouragement."

She slapped him on his rear.

He lurched forward but slowed to a stop when we reached the other horses. Try as I would, I could not get Shadrach to advance. Another round of encouragement from the instructor moved Shadrach reluctantly forward.

I was elated. *We're moving! I'm riding!*

But just as the train of horses was under way, Shadrach decided enough was enough. He shrugged. I fell on the ground, shaken but unhurt. He snorted in what seemed like obvious disgust at the presumption of this tinhorn who imagined she could ride him. I was mortified but relieved when the instructor said, "I think that's enough for one day."

She escorted me the short distance back to the stables, on foot.

Our next outing went pretty much the same way, despite some careful instruction about gripping with my knees. By that point my feelings for Shadrach were a jumble of fear, loathing, and a desperate need to be liked.

The third time I grimly, determinedly progressed a little farther before I renewed my acquaintance with the ground.

Somehow, though, by my fourth outing, I learned something about staying seated, and Shadrach resigned himself to my riding him. At last I experienced the full glory of a trail ride, albeit on a slouchy old one-eyed horse. I felt a new freedom, almost as if I were floating.

So began years of riding, first galloping over the bare brown pungent hills of home, then in the Sierras on a week-long pack trip with my parents when I was ten. Riding alone in the pristine wilderness, stopping beside an ice-blue mountain tarn at the edge of timberline, I experienced the high point of my childhood. Consumed by joy, I conjured a swirl of images—all the things that had happened to bring me to that glorious moment. And I thanked old Shadrach, who in his own way had taught me well.

It's your turn now

Further thoughts for readers, writers, and storytellers

Do you remember learning to ride a bike or a horse or learning to ski—how you failed at first and finally gained mastery? There may be a story worth sharing.

14: Stretch Makes His Point

As I watched the squirrels on my deck struggle with the bird-feeder's anti-squirrel mechanisms, I gained respect for their ingenuity when new obstacles were set before them. But I still filed them under "nuisances" in my mind.

Then, after one especially long and harsh winter, I found three squirrel corpses in our backyard. I realized getting at my bird feeder was more than idle entertainment for them—it was a case of life or death. After that day, when the ground where they buried their nuts froze solid, my husband and I scattered birdseed for them. Their disputes over the seed were just as entertaining as their attempts to defeat the most squirrel-proof feeder.

Yet I continued to underestimate them until another incident one sunny winter afternoon.

For some weeks I'd been watching squirrels flee the deck as I opened the deck door and let out my Welsh springer spaniel, Rufus—usually so I could refill the bird feeder. Rufus invariably but amiably chased the squirrels, clearing the deck for refueling.

When Rufus caught up with a squirrel, he drew back and let it escape. But the squirrels took his efforts seriously and scattered frantically. One particular squirrel regularly departed the deck by way of a pine tree branch that seemed impossibly far for him to reach. As he leapt and extended himself full length to reach the branch's tip, he seemed to fly. I wanted to photograph this remarkable feat from my back door, which gave me the best view.

Whenever I opened the back door Rufus rushed out and the raiding squirrels scattered. That's when my target squirrel, whom I named "Stretch," leapt from deck to tree. That's when I could take his picture. I hadn't mastered my new camera, though, so the result was always a blurred image. I repeated this action, over and over, shooting for the perfect photo in my mind's eye—but no joy. Stretch was too fast. Still, I kept trying.

One day, the squirrels were particularly persistent. So was I. I opened the door. The dog, predictably, rushed out. Stretch performed on cue, and I blurrily recorded the event. By the third time I pulled this trick, Stretch had had it. He leapt onto his branch from which he let out his pent-up feelings at me.

"Here you provide us with seeds, and then when we come to eat, you chase us away," he chittered at me, loudly, in tones I clearly understood. *"You are driving me crazy!"*

The remarkable thing about the outburst wasn't his irritation, but that he directed his anger at *me*, not at Rufus, who, he seemed to know, was just doing what dogs do. He somehow realized I was the source of his torment, so he gave me what my grandmother would have called "what for."

I was impressed. That squirrel was aware that other creatures had intent. He realized they shouldn't be judged for what they did (Rufus chasing squirrels without catching one) but for their motives (my disrupting the squirrels' mealtime for my own amusement.) This requires what animal behaviorists call a theory of mind: the squirrel could reason about unobservable mental states such as intentions and desires.

In the realm of animal psychology there is still little agreement on whether most animals have this capacity. But for me, Stretch provided an answer. He clearly was reasoning on a higher plane than I had seen in, say, Rufus. In his eyes, I was taunting him. And that, Stretch told me, is never appropriate.

It's your turn now

Further thoughts for readers, writers, and storytellers

Sometimes animals give you the eerie feeling that you are in the presence of a mind communicating with you as an equal. How did that make you feel? Share your story.

15: Rufus Delivers the Day

M any years ago, when I directed the religious education program in my congregation, I brought my Welsh springer spaniel, Rufus, to work with me during summer weekdays. As I worked, he peaceably waited at my feet until it was time to go out and romp on the ample grounds of our 1912 Georgian brick mansion.

Another weekday occupant of the building that summer was an Alzheimer's day-care group. Rufus, an old but healthy dog with a great love of people and food, followed his nose and discovered the group's routine: they ate hot meals at midday. He pulled hard on his leash when I took him for his lunchtime walk.

"Rufus!" I ordered. "Let's go outdoors!"

But he had other ideas, and his red-and-white body pulled me across the smooth marble floors toward the Terrace Room, which the group had rented. When we came to the glass doors, we immediately attracted the attention of the twenty clients and their group leaders. An attractive middle-aged woman, who seemed to be in charge, came to the door.

"I'm sorry to disturb you," I said. "I was taking my dog out for a walk, but we somehow ended up here."

Rufus wagged his stubby tail vigorously as he sniffed at the doorway.

"That's quite all right," the woman said, smiling at us. "Won't you come in and visit with us for a while? I'm Gail, the head of the program."

"And I'm Betsy. But I'm afraid he would disturb your clients while they are trying to eat their lunches."

"Not at all. They love having visitors. Do come in."

In we went. The elderly clients were arranged at long tables, each one with a hot meal in a tinfoil container with a cardboard lid. Some lids had already been removed, and some people had begun to eat. I saw a few startled faces, but for the most part we were met with smiles of delight. Rufus, in turn, was thrilled to discover so many new friends, all equipped with mouth-watering goodies. He panted and pulled on his leash.

"Why don't you walk up and down the tables and let each person greet him?" Gail suggested. I complied. As we walked, Rufus met each person with a brisk wag of his tail and an eager wriggle of his body. The few who were hesitant didn't deter him from moving on quickly to the next friendly face.

As we came to the end of the row, one elderly woman reached out with a small morsel of carved turkey in her hand. Rufus eagerly grabbed it, wolfed it down in one gulp, and returned to lick the woman's hand gratefully. I looked to Gail to see if this was okay. She nodded and smiled brilliantly. After that, everyone, even the initially reluctant, wanted to give Rufus some tidbit.

Gail said, "Why not put a few bits into a dish for him?" She picked up an empty tinfoil container and let the remaining clients contribute a bite from their own lunches. I limited the size of the offerings out of respect for Rufus's elegant figure.

Gail put the dish on the floor for Rufus, and he eagerly made for it. But there was a problem: the dish was so lightweight that when he went to take a bite, his muzzle pushed it forward. Everyone laughed as Rufus pushed that dish around the room in vain pursuit of his lunch.

Then a much-diminished man with curly white hair stood up and decisively moved to the dish, securing it with his two feet and abruptly bringing it to a halt. Rufus eagerly gulped down the food. In less than half a minute, it was gone. The entire room was festooned in smiles, and Rufus's savior looked as proud as a new father.

"Wonderful!" Gail said. "Dogs can have a magical effect on our clients. I hope you will stay until everyone has had a chance to pet him, and by all means, come again."

Then she whispered in my ear, "I would never have expected Mr. Davis to rescue Rufus. He hasn't said a word for two years and is usually quite withdrawn."

I felt chills run up my spine.

This was the first of Rufus's many visits to the Alzheimer's group. And every time, Mr. Davis stepped proudly forward to steady his dish.

It's your turn now

Further thoughts for readers, writers, and storytellers

Have you ever seen a pet work a transformation in someone's life, even your own? You can keep the magic going by writing or telling about it.

16: A Sermon on Mortality, with Squirrels

I've listened to, conducted, and participated in a great many memorable Sunday services at my church over fifty years. Yet it's so easy to forget exactly what was said in these memorable services.

A certain alchemy takes place between the speaker and the listener, a kind of dialogue that overlays our personal reactions onto the actual material of the service itself. Because of this alchemy, what is said is very often quite different from what is heard.

For me, the most spectacular example of this contradiction happened with Rev. Clark Olsen, our minister between 1968 and 1978. His particular passion was creative excellence in Sunday services, whether ministerial or lay-led. His motto was, "We can do more."

On one particular Sunday morning in 1977, more was done. Clark was to speak on "Dealing with Death" on a spectacularly beautiful early spring morning. A wet snow had fallen in the night, coating every branch and defining every twig with an inch of sparkling white crystals. Clark had arranged all the chairs to face the garden, so we could enjoy the dazzling snowy scene. He'd placed the portable lectern to one side of the windows, facing into the room.

In the trees, two squirrels chased each other up and down and across the landscape in a courtship ritual. They sprayed cascades of brilliant snow across our field of vision. Like us, they seemed delighted with the newly created wonderland. As we listened to the uplifting strains of Beethoven that began the service, the squirrels dashed back and forth across branches and electrical wires like circus aerialists.

Suddenly, in the middle of their high-wire act, one squirrel jumped onto a snowy transformer and—ZAP! In a flash, it was electrocuted. Its lifeless body plummeted to earth.

Just as Beethoven's solemn music swelled grandly to a close, Clark rose to speak about mortality. At least two of those present had no idea what had just occurred. One was Clark, preoccupied with his coming talk. The other was the remaining squirrel.

As Clark spoke about the mysteries of existence, the newly-widowed creature darted back and forth in obvious puzzlement, looking in vain for its erstwhile mate. The rest of us sat, stunned and silent.

Clark must have felt his words greatly affecting us. The sincerity of our response seemed to move him to new heights of eloquence.

As he warmed to his topic, the room got gradually darker. I looked questioningly at a friend, an electrical engineer sitting next to me. He gestured from the lights to the transformer outside and shrugged. *Of course!* The electrocution of the squirrel had damaged the transformer, causing a slow fadeout of the building's power.

Whatever the material cause, the spiritual effect was to heighten the impact of Clark's talk even further.

I'll never forget the lyrical intensity of his words as they rang out in the gradually dimming room, while the lone squirrel darted back and forth. On the other hand, no matter how hard I try, I can't remember a word he said.

It's your turn now

Further thoughts for readers, writers, and storytellers

Memory can enrich our lives or fail us. Can you remember a vivid incident missing certain crucial elements?

17: Rufus in the Willow Tree

My Welsh springer spaniel, Rufus, was a great greeter, full of sniffings and waggings for every person he met, but also a deliverer of memorable farewells to everyone who visited our home on House Road.

Like many dogs, he loved to chase squirrels, but was routinely foiled when the squirrels ran up tree trunks, leaving him wistfully whining at the base. When Rufus was a year old, it occurred to me he probably could climb the trunk of the big old willow in our front yard, which leaned at a 45-degree angle. After all, I had had a childhood dog who had figured out how to get out of our enclosed yard by climbing a similar tree that branched over the fence.

So, one day when Rufus had failed yet again in his pursuit of a squirrel who had run up the willow tree, I encouraged him to follow the nimble fellow up the trunk. Rufus was very doubtful about this idea.

"Go for it!" I said. "You can do it!"

Eventually, he lunged at the tree. To his great surprise, his claws dug in. Up he went. The squirrel was as surprised as he was, but easily climbed out on a branch too thin for Rufus to follow.

Rufus, having climbed out on the first horizontal branch, lost interest in the squirrel. Being out on the branch delighted him. The neighborhood children ran over.

"Look at that! Rufus climbed the willow tree!" they chorused enthusiastically. All this attention was not lost on Rufus, who took up a perfect dog-show pose, rear legs extended. (How he knew to do that mystifies me since he'd never been to a dog show. Maybe it was in his genes. His parents were certified American Kennel Club champions.) Or maybe he was just a natural show-off.

From then on, Rufus clambered up that tree whenever he thought someone was looking. When we had dinner guests, Rufus's talent was particularly evident. At the evening's end, as we said our farewells at the front door, he maneuvered himself through their legs, darted across the lawn and up the willow tree, where he took up his show-dog pose. As the guests turned to leave, they came face-to-face with this display and were suitably surprised.

"Oh my God! Your dog is up in the tree!" Further exclamations of praise and amazement followed, all of which gratified Rufus.

Eventually we moved to another home on the far side of Morristown. Rufus made the adjustment very well except for one thing: there was no leaning willow tree in the front yard. He made do: whenever guests departed, he ran onto the lawn and took up his show-dog pose. To his great disappointment, the guests paid no attention. They went on their way without noticing him.

He kept trying for some months, but eventually gave in to the obvious: his show days were over.

It's your turn now

Further thoughts for readers, writers, and storytellers

Ah, the inner life of pets! Each one is unique and has particular talents all its own. The more you pay attention to them, the more you will delight in their little ways. And they make great copy! See what you can remember.

18: A Honey Communion

Of all creatures, great and small, I have the greatest fondness for the honeybee.

It brings me most closely in touch with the religious principle most important to me: respect for the interdependent web of all existence. The bee does not weave a web, as the spider does, but it gathers nectar from hundreds of different sources. In this way, she brings together the blooming parts of our world, unifying them in a moment of encounter with our tongues.

At the Morristown (NJ) Unitarian Fellowship, when I was most active there, we honored this transformation in a ritual I called a "Honey Communion."

The church's honeybees, which produced the honey for our ritual, were ensconced in three beehives on the second-floor porch of our old brick mansion. Ping Chun, a researcher at Bell Labs and an amateur beekeeper, tended them as a favor to us.

During the late 1980s, I coordinated the Religious Education program at the Fellowship and realized I most wanted the children to learn about their intimate interrelationship with the Earth. So I started Earth Camp, a summer day camp on the Fellowship grounds. It was staffed by Fellowship parents who were professional teachers during the school year.

Earth Camp was held for two weeks every August. It drew our Fellowship children and many other kids from the wider community.

We had wonderful classes and field trips to sites like the Great Swamp, The Raptors' Trust, Hacklebarney State Park, and the Garbage Museum in the New Jersey Meadowlands. Five-year-olds through sixth-graders were involved. Counselors were juniors and seniors in high school. The end of camp was marked by a dinner, an evening performance staged by the children, a great bonfire under the tall trees, and overnight camping on the grounds.

The children loved the experience, as parents told me every day. One mother said that the following February, her seven-year-old son introduced himself to a new boy at school by proudly saying, "I'm Eddy. I go to Earth Camp."

The August days of camp were also a busy time in the beehives, which were dormant in the cold of late autumn, winter, and early spring. To gather all the nectar needed for the life of their hives, the worker bees drove themselves extra hard during the long summer hours of daylight. They seemed to know they needed to make extra supplies for the humans, too.

One camp goal was to teach the children that every particle of their bodies was made of earth, air and water, brought together in an amazing recipe called Life. And that everything in their world, even their plastic toys, was made from our precious Earth.

To help them understand one way Earth turns into Eddy or Emily, we brought in Ping Chun. He calmed the bees with smoke. The children, standing at a respectful distance, watched Ping move among the bees with calm assurance, not even flinching when, while removing some racks of honeycombs, he was stung several times. He took the honeycombed racks into the kitchen, loaded them into a separator, and spun them as the children watched. They loved taking turns at spinning the wheel that freed the honey from its waxen home. Of course, we left plenty of the honey in the hive for the bees' own use.

Afterward we served the children a special snack of honey on biscuits made by an Earth Camp mother.

As they ate their biscuits, we asked them to close their eyes and imagine the many transformations that Earth had made, right there on the Fellowship's grounds, to make their morning snack: The small seeds of many different plants had drawn power from the sun and soil. They had transformed themselves into trees and flowers. The bees had gathered nectar from them. The nectar, making its way through the bees' bodies, had undergone its own transmutation, which was deposited in the waxen honeycombs the bees created. Finally, in the honeycombs, the liquid was turned into the honey we were familiar with. Right then, even as they ate, that honey was turning into boys and girls as they played and laughed and learned at Earth Camp.

"Tonight when you kiss your parents good night," I told them, "the sweet energy from the honey will be part of that good night kiss."

As the children opened their eyes, we invited them to thank all the plants that had given them this ambrosial blessing. We had written the names of Fellowship flowers and trees on a piece of paper so they could easily follow along.

We thanked the paulownia tree at the entrance to the parking lot, which sheds its great purple flowers every spring.

We thanked the weeping cherry trees by the whispering wall, and the linden trees like the one by the front fence.

We thanked the rhododendrons and the mountain laurels that grew by the oval entranceway, and the flowers that bloomed in the garden beside the Meeting Room.

We thanked the tomato and squash blossoms from the children's own vegetable garden, the chrysanthemums we put by the front doors in fall, and the humble clover that bloomed in the summer lawns.

Most importantly, we thanked the honeybees that had turned the nectar into honey and the beekeeper who had gathered the rich harvest.

Then we shut our eyes again and breathed in all we had received. Our minds swooped like so many bees around the Fellowship grounds. Then we breathed out our gratitude three times.

As we ate and imagined and breathed our thanks, we came together as one. That was our honey communion, though we never used that word "communion" with the children. That's just how I thought of it.

After our snack the children learned about the complex communication system bees use to let each other know where to find nectar. We played the Bee Dance Game in the rooms of the mansion.

"We're not smart enough to understand the complicated directions about routes and distance that bees give each other, merely by waggling their rear ends," I said. "So we made up directions of our own."

With little arrow signs on guides' rear ends to lead them, the children ran from the Meeting Room to the Great Hall to the Terrace Room and back to the Library in search of a bouquet of flowers. All the rear-end waggling produced a medley of giggles.

We always saved plenty of honey to have a honey communion with the congregation during a Sunday service every fall. We served homemade loaves of bread, which we tore into small pieces and laid out on trays, adding a dollop of honey to each. We told people about our bee adventure at camp, and then shared our thoughts about what we owed the Earth and the flowers, shrubs, and trees—and especially the bees—on the Fellowship's own grounds.

Then, as the trays were passed around and we each partook of the bread, we meditated on this bounty and its role in the interdependent web of existence.

Sad to say, we eventually had to remove the beehives from our property because of children with bee allergies. But when I think of the most meaningful food I ever ate, I remember the honey we took in gratitude from our Fellowship bees and shared with the children of Earth Camp. And I wonder, do those now-grown children still carry with them a memory of that encounter?

It's your turn now

Further thoughts for readers, writers, and storytellers

Can you recall something you ate once that made a particularly strong impression on you, and why? Tell us what made it special.

19: Barking at Death

What to make of a bird that refuses to move? Ringo wonders. In his eight years of life, he has never encountered this before.

The titmouse lies, belly up, beside the glass deck door that broke its neck. Cavalier King Charles Spaniels, I have read, are the dog breed furthest away from wolves in their DNA. That dry fact is very visible as Ringo comes face to face with death. No instinct prods him to mouth this songbird, which he used to chase from the bird feeder before he learned we protected them and they were not to be disturbed.

He stands above the titmouse warily, ready to dart away, thinking perhaps this is some trick of the little creature, who might just leap up and peck at him—who knew? He visibly trembles in fear through his black and white fur. When a dog can approach a bird like this, the natural order of things as he knows them has been violated.

Gradually, some courage comes to him, and he decides, in effect, to nag the bird into remembering its birdiness, hopping up, and flying away. He barks once. Seeing it has no effect, he barks again and again, all attention focused on rousing the little corpse.

Faced with the failure of his plan, he looks expectantly at me as I watch through the glass deck door, thinking I will resolve this enigma. But I do not rush to his aid. Though he cocks his ears at me in a beguiling way, he gets no response. So he resumes barking, plumed tail wagging frantically to show he means no harm.

In time, my husband goes out and gathers up the tiny body in a plastic bag and takes it to the garbage cans. Though the barking stops, Ringo does not give up his vigil. He circles and circles the spot, nose to the ground, knowing there is something important to understand there, but having no clue to the puzzle. The next night, at the same time, he returns to the spot, sniffs it, and barks some more. For his sake, I regret that he has no wolfish howl in his vocabulary to properly express his inexplicable experience.

When you unravel the mystery, little dog, I hope you will let me know. Truth to tell, I am as baffled as you by ultimate stillness.

It's your turn now

Further thoughts for readers, writers, and storytellers

Watching our pets respond to the world, you may find that you have a lot in common. What have you learned about your interconnectedness from observing your dog, your cat, your guinea pig? Watch closely, make notes, and write it down.

20: O, Freedom

"Stay away from the horse," the lake's lifeguard admonished through his megaphone. Obediently, the children on the sand receded toward their mothers on their bright beach towels.

I turned toward a shining vision: a light bay beauty, bridled and saddled in the English fashion, cantered freely across the wide expanse of beachside lawn. He was trained to obey every whim of his rider's will, but that day, on his own, his bright black plumes of mane and tail flying, he seemed to feel his liberation.

At first there was no sign of his master. The gelding stretched his legs into a joyous gallop and ran as if forever over the greensward.

In time, though, they appeared: a rider, dressed in jodhpurs, light whip in one hand, a stable manager, and two handlers. They fanned out across the lawn, faces anxious and arms outstretched as if to gather in the glory of this sight.

But to no avail. If this great animal wished to run, then run he would, turning in wide circles, moving freely from pace to pace. In the end, called by the sweet grasses, he slowed. He stretched down to eat, thereby allowing himself to be returned to the mastery of the bit.

He was led away. Yet still, in memory, he remained a symbol of liberty for all who recognize their bonds.

It's your turn now

Further thoughts for readers, writers, and storytellers

Sometimes, if you can identify with an animal, it can teach the meaning of what you have or even what you have lost. Tell the story of such a lesson you have learned.

IV: Watching the Wild Ones

21: Dancing with Whales

S enior Ditch Day: even the name had an adventurous, racy sound to it when I was in high school. Every year, for four years past, we younger girls had watched the seniors drop everything and, with whoops of delight, escape the confines of our girls' school and experience the independent pleasures of the wider world. The next day they returned, mysterious smiles on their faces, determined not to reveal the secrets of their day off.

Finally, it was our turn for this rite of passage. We deliberated where to go and decided on Montara Beach, just south of Half Moon Bay on the San Francisco peninsula. We jammed into a bus and headed south.

The water's edge didn't offer us the frolic in sunlit surf we had imagined. After all, this was May in northern California. The shore was dreary, cold, windy, and, of course, deserted. We gathered driftwood for a campfire and then huddled around it, gloomily wondering how we could salvage anything from the ruins of our expectations.

Looking around, we saw our section of beach was set in a cove, sheltered from the wildest waves of the Pacific Ocean. Because of the insistent wind that day, the water was choppy. It almost looked like something moved in the cove. We speculated we'd seen a sea turtle's flipper.

We were watching the water carefully when suddenly a vertical plume of water rose up. Then came a flash of something dark—a whale! No, *whales!* We sat, stunned and silent, as a pod of six or eight California gray whales headed straight for the shore near us.

After a minute's shock, I took on the responsibility (how typical) of ensuring these creatures did not get stranded. I scrambled to my feet and ran down to the water's edge, shouting and waving my arms. My classmates remained by the campfire, calling warnings after me.

Ignoring them, I came face to face with the lead whale. How utterly Other it was, its great ten-foot-tall head resting on the sand. Vast encrustations of barnacles camouflaged its features. It towered over me as I darted and whooped around its head, gesticulating urgently.

I shouted past its great jutting jaw at its forehead. Then I noticed its eye was below my own eye level and about ten feet beyond its front end. As I stared into its round dark globe, I felt exposed, as if this were the ultimate eye, as if I'd never truly been seen before that moment.

The other whales moved up onto the beach in rapid succession. I ran between them, hoping to find an ear to yell into, and looked forty feet out to sea where their enormous tails lashed from side to side in the surf. *If one of them rolls over on me, I thought, I'm a goner— but what a way to go!*

Suddenly, I realized that the beauty and drama of that moment had shattered my fears and inhibitions. I went more or less mad, abandoning myself to the experience, warbling and dancing among them as they rolled and heaved in the shallows. I stopped trying to get them to do anything and participated in that joyful encounter. Time passed in a great radiance of delight.

At last, whether motivated by my gyrations or just because they'd done what they came for, they quietly, simultaneously, melted back into the sea, leaving the beach as deserted as before, and leaving me in wonder.

This Ditch Day adventure was a parable of experiences to come—begun with bright expectations, often dashed, but just as often highlighted with amazing transformational encounters with people, animals, places, and ideas. And though I don't know all their stories, I imagine it has been true for my classmates, as well.

So this is my wish for them, and for us all: that as our own life adventures continue, when we find ourselves alone on those deserted, windy beaches of life, may we always find our whales.

It's your turn now

Further thoughts for readers, writers, and storytellers

Looking back over the encounters of your lifetime, is there one which, all unexpectedly, seems to stand out as a metaphor for your life? As you write in detail about this episode—its sights and textures, what was said or unsaid, expectations and reactions—you may learn more about the depth and meaning of your own life experience.

22: Song of the Walrus

Frankly, I wasn't expecting much from my trip to the New York Aquarium at Coney Island. My grown-up daughter, Jessica, had persuaded my husband Stefan and me to go with her for her birthday. I was not, at that time, a great lover of fish, so I perked up considerably when I saw the walrus exhibit.

The three walruses were housed in quarters which humans deem comfortable, if not luxurious. (No one, as far as I know, has asked the walruses.) In an outdoor area, they swam and basked on rocks. In an enclosed area, visitors watched their antics through the glass walls of the underwater tank.

As we approached the tank, all three walruses were swimming in the area. They lacked the long tusks I'd seen in pictures of wild walruses. (We later learned their tusks were filed off to prevent fatal infections caused by banging into the glass walls.)

I don't know why I imagined these zoo animals might pay me any attention. They got thousands of visitors a day and were likely overstimulated, if not downright jaded. Indeed two of them soon swam off, leaving us with one walrus. We solicited its attention.

I reached out and rubbed the glass in a circular motion. The walrus swam to the glass wall and rubbed against it in what I would call a suggestive manner. (At that point I assumed it was a *he*). This drew laughter from the small crowd around us. I responded, I blush to say, by rubbing my shoulder against the glass.

Immediately he rubbed *his* shoulder against my portion of the glass. It was clear to all a courtship had begun. This point was underlined by what happened next. The walrus played with something resembling an elongated rubbery baseball bat: he put one end into his mouth and sucked on it. It was a long moment before I realized he was playing with a part of his own anatomy. (I learned later walrus males are the most gifted of any creature in that department.)

Just then a mother with young children showed up to witness this display. One of the children pointed.

"Oh look, Mommy!" she said loudly. "What is that walrus playing with?"

"Never mind, honey," said the mother, with a hasty yank on her daughter's arm. "We have to hurry up."

One of the other walruses, who I assumed was a female, returned to the courtship site and slammed into the glass, a piece of body language clearly directed at me, as if to say, *Quit tormenting this poor guy. Don't you think he's had enough?*

I did grudgingly think the female walrus had a point. So, after a few cooling-off maneuvers, making apologies to the now-clearly-male walrus, our family moved to the outdoor section of the enclosure. Having formed such a coherent connection with two walruses in such a short time, I found myself hooked on these whiskered pinnipeds.

Before long the male walrus surfaced in the area farthest from where we stood. I thought he would not spot me since walruses have little beady eyes that seem to want prescription lenses. I was wrong. Within a few minutes, he had somehow zeroed in on me (I'm guessing it was my red plaid shirt) and galumphed across the enclosure in my direction.

It's no small thing when a one-ton amorous walrus galumphs toward you. Since the enclosure was discreetly walrus-proofed, he was forced to stop twenty feet from me. He gave me a look of longing I would not have expected to see on his Teddy-Rooseveltish countenance.

But then came the pièce de résistance: he opened his fleshy lips in a delicate "O" and sang me his walrus courtship song. It was not the full-fledged, complex walrus courtship song that males sing to females in the wild, for he had never heard such a song, but then, neither had I. It consisted of a single, high-pitched note of ineffable yearning.

I was entirely carried away by its purity, and fascinated by the demure shade of pink that lined his lips as he crooned. I was a woman of more than a certain age, and it had been a long time since anyone had approached me with that kind of originality. I admit I was flattered. I responded, by pure misguided instinct, with what sounded like a wolf howl. He did not seem discouraged.

He continued his one-note song with great earnestness for some time as I listened, enthralled—until two young women passed behind us and stopped for a moment.

"Oh, look," one said to the other. "There's your boyfriend—at it again."

Had I even imagined that I was the one true object of this walrus's affections? If so, the spell was truly broken. The idea that he carried on with whoever passed by was a bit much for my ego.

I broke things off as gracefully as I could and searched for a walrus expert who could explain some of what we had experienced. We tracked down the keeper, who explained the three walruses consisted, as we had supposed, of two females and a male, all adolescents. They had been rescued from the Arctic Ocean, where Inuit natives had slaughtered their mothers when they were born—an annual practice allowed by treaty.

The infants were subsequently hand-raised at the New York Aquarium.

The male was, as we had observed, coming into sexual maturity. The females, however, would not come into estrus for another few months. While they were not at all responsive to his advances, they were aware enough to be jealous of his regular attempts to attract women.

"How often does he approach women?" I asked.

"Oh, pretty regularly—every afternoon between three and five."

Now my daughter piped up. She'd been watching these goings-on with a great but silent glee that now found expression:

"Don't feel bad, Mom," she said. "He was courting *you* at a quarter of *six*."

It's your turn now

Further thoughts for readers, writers, and storytellers

Have you ever encountered a zoo or aquarium animal whose behavior was unusual? How did you respond, and what happened next? You may have a good story there.

23: Eating in Jockey Hollow

During the American Revolution in 1779–1780, the worst winter of the century, General George Washington installed his troops at Jockey Hollow in Morristown, New Jersey. The suffering was great, but you wouldn't have known it on one particular weekday afternoon in the late fall of 1991. The leafless woods were full of peace—the peace the soldiers must have dreamed of as they tossed and turned through cold and hungry nights.

Surrounded by November stillness, I ate my bread and cheese at a picnic table provided by Morristown National Historical Park. And I thought of them.

Abruptly, a red-tailed hawk swooped down into a nearby bare treetop, his talons gripping a dead rabbit. He turned his head this way and that, alert for interventions. Apparently concluding I posed no risk to his lunchtime plans, he settled down to his feast. His beak tore pelt from flesh, muscle from tendon, as he disassembled a life.

Just as abruptly, a school bus roared up and stopped almost directly under the hawk's tree, hastily disgorging a load of small children, complete with chaperones, and roared off again. The children swarmed over the remaining picnic tables till all benches were occupied.

Adults shouted directions. No one said, "Be still and look around you. See what you can see." Instead children traded food, scrapped, ate, and were as full of themselves as they could be.

The hawk watched this hubbub with surprising patience and then flew off, his wings casting an unnoticed shadow across the tables. *There are better places to eat a rabbit*, he seemed to say to the woods.

Children and teachers finished eating, the school bus reappeared, and a new flurry of instructions was uttered. Half-eaten lunches were stuffed into the provided receptacles, and everyone climbed back into the school bus without so much as a glance around. The bus lumbered off.

I was left alone again, eating my apple amid the November quiet of the leafless woods, thinking of George Washington's soldiers, of the school bus and its occupants, the red-tailed hawk and the dead rabbit. The next time I am in a crowd of people, all full of their own purposes, I hope an inner voice says to me, *"Be still and look around you. See what you can see."*

It's your turn now

Further thoughts for readers, writers, and storytellers

So let that be your mission: "Be still and look around you. See what you can see."

24: It's All Happenin' at the Bronx Zoo

A great silverback, lord of his domain, lounged against the base of a tree a mere yard from me. Clearly, though, I was not uppermost in his mind.

Only a few weeks before, he and his troop of females and young had taken over the new gorilla quarters. He knew already that the sturdy pane of glass between us would keep me at a good arm's length. I was just part of a changing picture on his wall.

Indifferent to visitors' antics, the silverback ignored my feeble attempts to win his attention. Even with tourist traffic coming and going before him, he sat in solitude as profound as if he'd trained for it in a Tibetan lamasery.

One of his females, skittering along on her knuckles, approached. Once settled into his arms, she told her tale of woe. She had a boo-boo on her forehead, a light abrasion the size of a fifty-cent piece that shone red against her black skin.

The silverback was startled out of his ruminations. *Troubles? What troubles? Ah, I see.* While cradling her—oh so gently—in one arm, he reached with the other to inspect—oh so delicately—the boo-boo. She submitted to his touch.

He examined her with focused intensity. It was as if he'd never seen a scrape before, as if this were indeed the First Scrape, and he the first of all investigators into harm.

He brought his finger thoughtfully to his lips, then his tongue, and tasted the warm, salty blood. Suddenly, he looked upward with knitted brows, as if stricken by a memory, perhaps of an injury of his own, and how it had hurt. He seemed to ponder the significance of it all.

He thought for a long time. Perhaps he thought about how the skin feels fine, but just underneath the skin is a world of feeling terrible, and how should that be so? Or maybe he thought about something else entirely.

He continued to comfort his companion with one arm, but his gaze was lost in space and time, perhaps in the meaning of pain and grief. After a while, just to remind himself, he again touched and tasted the wound and fell into solemn contemplation. And so he continued for the better part of a half hour.

I thought if I stayed there long enough I would understand what that gorilla was thinking. The longer I stayed, the more it seemed his cogitations might be as worthy as those of philosophers through the ages who have considered the mystery of suffering.

Then, at some unspoken signal, the episode ended. The female felt sufficiently consoled and returned to the hillside from which she came. The silverback, having either thought through the issue or given up in frustration, undertook an exploratory tour of the enclosure.

So I, also done with deep thinking, set off to see the exhibit where butterflies fluttered to the music of Vivaldi.

It's your turn now

Further thoughts for readers, writers, and storytellers

You have seen primates at the zoo. Have you experienced the commonality of tenderness, of suffering, of so many emotions, between us and our relatives? Go again, look closely, and write.

25: The Osprey Nest

For Francis and Eleanor Blanchard, my
parents, who lost two babies before me.

Two white-headed, black-robed hawks build their nest on a high platform, just forty feet from my vacation window on Florida's west coast. The male and female fetch sticks and moss and palm fronds to build the giant nest. As they come and go, they call to one another. Daily, they stand on the nest's edge to mate and seal their commitment. It's a good spot—bay waters move musically nearby, and a cooling breeze softens oppressive air.

At first, they prosper. Two eggs are laid and hatched. The male fetches fish for all to share. Then he falls ill and cannot fish--has he ingested plastic? The young go unfed. The female seems unable to take his place. The fledglings tire of ceaseless begging and slump down in the nest. They die.

After a time, the male recovers, but the breeding season is far advanced. Is there time? When he returns to the nest, he hears the female's cries.

"Shall we try again, then?" he seems to ask.

She does not call out, only holding herself very still.

It's your turn now

Further thoughts for readers, writers, and storytellers

People and animals alike experience the full cycle of life. Can you remember a birth or death, in nature or in your family circle, which was especially significant?

26: Eyes and Ears at the Anchorage Zoo

I came to this rescue zoo in Anchorage to make closer acquaintance with creatures whose cousins I knew in the wild—injured bald eagles, wolves and Dahl sheep, orphaned moose and captive-bred caribou.

Passing by the wolf enclosure, a woman remarked to me, "I wish it would stop drizzling like this and either flat-out rain or quit. This in-between is driving me crazy." A wolf stalking past just then shot back, *Let it rain. Then none of your kind would come at all.*

One bald eagle was more patient with me. Having been rescued after a near-fatal collision with a power line, he seemed to know this was the afterlife and accepted his fate with aplomb.

I am still wild, he told me, *still the king.*

The tigers, though, ruled uneasily over their seemingly ample domain.

Yes, we are monarchs here, they said as they slouched down the trail beside the fence. *But what maddens us more than fences are the searching eyes from the other side that strike like arrows and pierce our souls. We spend our days trying to dodge these arrows, but they find us every day. I could bear the fences if it weren't for the eyes.*

The Alaska Zoo is a rescue zoo, with high ideals. I'm sure it's a fine one. But I think my zoo days are over.

My hearing has grown too acute with age.

It's your turn now

Further thoughts for readers, writers, and storytellers

Zoos can be a rich source of encounters—if you can bear what you learn. Listen carefully for what is unspoken. You may discover something unexpected.

V: Adventuring with David

27: Meeting the Mountain Man

When I met David Schooley, I did not dream he would open a new world of adventure for me.

He was "my yard man," as my mother-in-law, Joyce, called him when I first met him. He came from time to time.

"Not often enough," she complained.

But, by fits and starts, he helped her convert her one-acre garden to shrubs and beds of native plants. As a founder of the California Native Plant Society, she was happy with the results.

David was a tall, bearded, strawberry blond of about fifty. His clothes were shaggy. His face was permanently reddened by the sun, and his hands showed clear evidence of hard labor with the soil. He talked little, but when he came to the house for some iced tea, I noticed that his speech was halting.

I asked Joyce about this.

"David has a hard story," she told me later, as we settled into work on a jigsaw puzzle. "His parents go way back with Doc [her husband] and me. We were in graduate school together and moved to California at about the same time after the war. You know them."

She named a couple I had often met. David's father was a speechwriter for the president of the University of California. His mother was a modern dance instructor.

"David was working in construction about a decade ago when a load of bricks fell on his head," Joyce continued. "He was in a coma for three months and had to learn to walk and talk all over again. He is blind in one eye and is left, as you can hear, with speech problems. But he is still getting better."

"How sad," I said. "But what an odd combination—the son of a PhD, working in construction."

"Well, that's Berkeley," Joyce sighed. "It had that effect on lots of kids of his generation. Anti-war, pro-pot, you know. David was brilliant—very advanced for his age, always—but he didn't finish college. David loves a good fight, and what with the Vietnam War and nuclear weapons, he was swept up in protest movements. They came before a career. He's still protesting."

"What's on the agenda these days?"

I had never been involved in protest movements, having graduated just before the upheavals at Berkeley in the '60s.

"In college he became interested in environmental studies. Before his accident made him disabled, he discovered San Bruno Mountain, near the San Francisco airport, and found his life's work—looking after the mountain."

"How do you look after a mountain?"

"Because San Francisco's smelly garbage dump was nearby, San Bruno Mountain was never developed when the rest of the peninsula filled in. When the city moved the dump, developers swarmed around, but they didn't reckon with the force of David's determination to preserve what was the last remnant of native ecosystem remaining on the peninsula—a reminder of what San Francisco was once like, before modern civilization moved in."

"How could one man make a difference?"

"Remember, he'd taken part in a lot of protest movements while at Berkeley. He organized local people who wanted the mountain preserved, and he continued the battle when others' interest flagged, never for a moment giving way. Eventually his organization, San Bruno Mountain Watch, won the battle to create San Bruno Mountain State and County Park on one part of the land. But then they found that land outside the boundaries sheltered rare and endangered species of butterflies, so the fight to preserve *that* land began. Oh, and by the way, he also weeds the mountain."

"You can't weed a mountain."

"If you are David Schooley and determined to keep out non-native plants that are destroying the ecosystem, you will. Of course, in the long run the developers will win their battles, and non-native plants will win theirs. It's only a matter of time. No one man can do what he is attempting, especially with his injuries."

"So he works nonstop to save this mountain, and he does yard work. What does he do in his spare time?"

Joyce smiled.

"He writes poetry, takes photographs, and draws. His subject is always the mountain, and he uses his creations to arouse people's interest, especially groups of schoolchildren that he takes on hikes."

The next time I saw David, I stopped to talk.

"Joyce has told me a lot about you and your work to save the mountain," I said. "When I was growing up in Berkeley, I spent every Saturday in the hills, hiking with my father. I miss those hills so much now."

"I used to hike in the Berkeley hills every Saturday, too, when I was little," he said, leaning on his rake. "For me, they will always be the beautiful hills of home."

He spoke somewhat haltingly, with a childlike simplicity that was nevertheless poetic.

"Want to come on a hike with me sometime?" he asked.

I was amazed he could fit me in, but I hesitated.

"I doubt I could keep up with you."

"I walk slowly, too. That way I see more."

"Okay, let's go, then. Just let me know where and when. But I am only in the Bay Area for a few days more."

"Tomorrow I am hiking on Mount Montara on the San Francisco peninsula to take some photos. Come along."

With some trepidation I agreed. I picked him up in Brisbane, where he lived, for the drive to Mount Montara. On our way, he asked me why I happened to be in California.

"My mother has been an invalid for 20 years now," I explained, "so even though I live in New Jersey I come out often to look after her and help out my father. Since my husband's parents live nearby, I also spend some time with them."

"I remember your husband, Stefan, from when we were kids. He was a good egg."

"It's wonderful that he doesn't mind these trips I have to make to look after my mother," I said. "He *is* a good egg. One flaw, though—he doesn't enjoy hiking or camping, so this is a real treat for me."

When we reached the mountain, we set out to climb. Not to the top, David explained, but to a grove of manzanita trees. It would be an easy two-hour hike suitable for someone out of practice.

"I love manzanitas," I said. "I always think their smooth, shiny red-brown bark almost looks like human skin. I haven't seen any in a long time."

"Well then, let's go."

He turned, lifted his backpack to his shoulders, and set off uphill, choosing a path through a dense scrubland of stunted wild brush. Looking around, I saw the terrain got more rainfall and heavy fog near the ocean than the dusty Berkeley hills. The landscape was lusher, too.

David walked at a measured pace I could almost keep up with. Once in a while he paused for me to catch up and pointed out the names of flowering plants or fragrant bushes. The weather was sunny and cool, with a slight breeze. My windbreaker was quite adequate protection. I loved falling into the easy rhythm of the trail hike.

"Here we are," he finally announced. Before us was a lovely grove of manzanita trees, growing amid very rocky terrain. Each tree, only about eight feet high, looked as though a Japanese gardener had pruned it. Each branch angled off in a way to please the strictest aesthete. The red-skinned branches shone in the afternoon sunlight.

David busied himself with taking pictures.

"This is a magical, mystical Montara manzanita grove," he said, enjoying the way the words rolled off his tongue. "Look around you to find out why."

"What am I looking for?"

"I won't tell you. Look high and low."

I searched the trees, the ground, and rocks underneath, enjoying the pure beauty of every viewpoint, loving the way boulders and mosses and madrone shrubs gracefully underlay the grove.

After a while, I saw an object in a tree branch. About eight inches long, it had a curved shape resembling one arm of a double helix, as in a DNA molecule. When I took it down from the tree, I saw it was made of cast bronze and resin and was carved with an inscription.

"Overture," it said. "Walk San Pedro Valley Park Trails—Pacifica, California. Brooks Creek Trail Manzanita Grove." It was signed "Lou Pearson. 11-6-1992."

It had been made only a week before! The artist also had engraved an outline sketch of the mountain range, as seen from that vantage point.

"That's a really beautiful one," said David. "If we keep looking around, now that you know what you are looking for, I bet you'll find more."

Before long, we had found several of different sizes, each with its own name, but all of the same distinctive shape. We left them in place, but I held onto my original find.

"He put these sculptures out here for people to discover and take home," David explained. "I know Lou Pearson. He told me that he dreamed this shape. He woke up knowing that he was supposed to make these objects. He casts them himself."

"What does the shape signify?"

"It means peace and oneness and preserving the Earth."

"So he has created a sculpture garden on the mountain?"

"He puts these sculptures out here to inspire people to work for those causes. You can take one home to New Jersey, if you promise to be inspired."

He twinkled at me, but I knew he was serious.

"I have founded and run Earth Camp, an environmental summer day camp in New Jersey," I said. "So you can see I'm already inspired."

As we rested among the manzanita trees, we fell into a long conversation about the importance and joy of teaching children about the natural world.

"Introducing children to wildness—it's soooo vital. They are the ones, the future," he said.

As we talked I felt our friendship growing as if from the moist soil of the mountainside.

Remember Joyce's remark that David was bound to fail in his efforts to save the mountain from further development? Since 1969, when he began, David has lost some battles but won others. After 40 years, San Bruno Mountain Watch had an office, a director who oversees the activities of dozens of volunteers, and a nursery for the propagation of native plants to be placed on the mountain and around the area. David turned to cutting trails and, along with many others, leading regular hikes.

And, oh, yes, teams of people weed the mountain.

It's your turn now

Further thoughts for readers, writers, and storytellers

Through David, I learned a lot about the power of perseverance. Have you ever encountered people who turn their backs on the conventions of society, and yet, through their unique vision and effort, accomplish a lot? What may you have learned from them?

28: Besh and Thelma Lived in a Tree

B efore I met David Schooley, I'd seen San Bruno Mountain dozens of times as I drove from the airport toward San Francisco. The big expanse of hilly grassland had made me wonder, *Why had this one piece of open country stayed free in this huge, densely developed metropolitan area,* while neighboring lands were paved over with little ticky-tacky houses?

Eventually, I had learned the answer: David, my husband's boyhood friend had founded, led, and perpetuated a movement to save the mountain as public land, forever. He, and the volunteers he had inspired, had managed to get preserved the largest native ecosystem within any major metropolitan area in the nation.

But then he faced another challenge—saving rare and endangered species of butterflies on adjoining unpreserved land. So the struggle was ongoing.

One particular day, David left behind the battles—the endless petitions, ballot initiatives, and paperwork—and took me to meet Besh and Thelma and see their tree home. We drove to the parking lot of an industrial building on the outskirts of Brisbane, parked, and started up the northeast side of the mountain. Grassland gave way to scrub and trees. Every late afternoon, waves of fog flowing over the Franciscan landscape provided nourishment to the landscape.

David walked ahead of me, climbing with slow, purposeful steps. Out of shape, I scrambled to keep up. After a half-mile climb, we entered Owl Canyon and neared the outer edge of a huge old live-oak tree. Its branches, dipping down and rising up again, extended forty feet in all directions from its enormous trunk.

On the far side of the tree, a nice trickle of fresh spring water emerged from the ground and flowed gently down the hill. On the western side, from which we had approached, the ground was fairly clear. On the uphill side of the tree, though, a curious jumble of fiberglass, plastic sheeting, and tarp had been cobbled together to make a roof and walls. Branches were used as roof timbers. About three feet up the trunk of the tree, where it first branched out, was an entranceway between gnarled branches. Looking backward from this vantage point, we could see San Francisco and the sparkling bay in the distance.

"Come on," David urged me.

"But what about Besh and Thelma?" I asked. "We can't just walk into their home."

"They don't mind when I show people around. They aren't here right now because they've had a scare. They've moved out for the time being. But this is where they normally live. Come on in."

He ushered me up the trunk and into their one-room residence.

The home was very much a collaboration among earth, tree, and people. The floor and walls of the tidy room were made of tamped-down earth, as was the fireplace. Thelma, who came from Honduras, knew how to prepare the dirt so it would not turn to mud in winter and dust in summer.

The living branches of the tree served as structural elements—for a yard-long bookcase, other shelving, and a sofa whose base was molded out of earth. The sofa seat was made from old planking, and the floor was covered by a raggedy Persian rug—a dumpster rescue, David told me. Next to the fireplace, at a good height for cooking, pots and pans hung from a horizontal branch passing through.

"Whoever designed this place must have been an architect at heart," I said. "Everything fits so perfectly."

"The tree house was originally built by a hermit named Dwight. When he moved out I offered the place to Besh, who had been living in the San

Francisco garbage dump near Candlestick Park. I suggested that if he moved here, he could take care of Owl Canyon."

"Why does Owl Canyon need taking care of?"

"Because of the invasive foreign plants like Scotch broom and fennel that have come here from Europe and elsewhere. They are practically taking over the mountain from the native plants, which native animals and insects depend on. One by one, the invasive species have to be weeded out. It's a huge job. Besh is very good at tending to Owl Canyon. He and Thelma got married soon after he moved here. She's a big help."

"But don't other people bother them?"

"When they hear people approaching, if they don't want to be seen, they hide—down here."

David lifted the sofa seat and revealed the entrance to a large underground cavity. He stepped into it. In a moment, he had disappeared. I was alone in the tidy, snug room. Moments later, he was back again.

"The sleeping quarters and chemical toilet are in a separate area just up the hillside," he explained. "Now let's go meet Besh and Thelma."

Off we went, back down toward my car. In an instant, the house in Owl Canyon had passed out of sight.

Once in the car, we drove to an entirely different part of the mountain—a steep, grassy hillside bisected by a fast-moving highway. David had me pull over to the side of the road and park. As we got out of the car, he swept up an armload of fresh fruits and vegetables from the back seat.

"They're too far from the grocery store to restock regularly, so I bring them a few things when I come," he explained. He plunged sure-footedly over what seemed to be a precipice.

"Wait for me," I protested. "I can never climb down that slope."

"Then come down on your behind," he called as he disappeared around a bend.

I hastily sat down and tried to scoot down on the rocky grasslands. I managed to get the twenty feet down at the cost of ripping the seat out of my jeans. At the bottom was a narrow trail leading almost immediately to a small ledge, where a tent was pitched precariously.

David was already handing over groceries to Thelma, a dark-haired woman whom I judged to be in her late thirties. Besh, an older man with glasses and graying hair, was putting a kettle on a camp stove. They greeted me warmly and offered me a seat on an old paint bucket.

While Besh made us tea, I explained my jeans mishap. Everyone laughed. We had a pleasant visit, but they clearly were uncomfortable in their current quarters and longing to get back home to Owl Canyon, which Besh called "a little piece of paradise."

After we made our way back to the car, I asked David what had driven Besh and Thelma from their tree house to this uneasy mountainside perch. He explained that Besh had discovered a patch of marijuana being cultivated in the canyon and had ripped it out. He was afraid the people who had planted it would take revenge on him and Thelma, either by harming them or reporting them to the authorities who supervised the park where the tree was located.

Eventually, Besh and Thelma returned to Owl Canyon and lived there happily for another decade. I visited them several times. Over the years David took generations of schoolchildren to visit the couple in their tree house, telling them that Besh and Thelma were good stewards of the land.

Inevitably, I suppose, the law caught up with the two homesteaders. They were evicted from their "little piece of paradise," which, after all, belonged to the county. Their amazing home was completely demolished, leaving the old oak tree to its former solitude.

To my way of thinking, a replica of this tree house should be erected in the Smithsonian Museum as an example of people who lived peacefully and usefully "outside the box" of modern American civilization.

It's your turn now

Further thoughts for readers, writers, and storytellers

Some people live in amazing places, whether elegant mansions or seaside shacks. You might like to recall and even write about your encounter with such a spot and the people who lived there.

29: The Pack Rat's Ways

In the early 1990s David Schooley took me to his favorite secret campsite on the San Francisco Peninsula. The Pacific Ocean was close enough that we could hear elephant seals barking when the wind blew just right, but it was far enough away that the Ohlone Native Americans, who once inhabited the site, trekked several miles to reach it. They left their seashell remnants on the campsite, mixed with the local soil.

Deeply secluded in trees and brush, it was a perfect spot for a camp. A small creek flowed through it. A swath of nearly flat cleared land adjoined the creek bed. Civilization, with its discontents, had begun to encroach on the general area. So far, though, this small slice of heaven was undisturbed. David did all he could to see it remained so.

We parked at a distance and backpacked in, approaching from different angles every time so no telltale track pointed the way.

Presiding over our site was a great old bay tree, which hosted a pack rat's nest, or midden, in its branches. A pack rat is also known as a wood rat, but I preferred the somewhat obsessive quality of the former name, which made me, a cluttery collector, feel as if I knew her already.

Pack rats have few natural defenses from predators, so their best recourse is to remain elusive. Over time, I spent many days and nights at the campsite without catching more than a single glimpse of the pack rat herself. One day in the late afternoon, I saw her mount the tip of a bay-tree branch growing low and parallel to the ground. She traveled thirty feet toward the trunk and then up and into the entrance of the midden.

She resembled the urban rat in outline, except for her large, round Mickey Mouse ears that weren't at all rat-like. Taken with this discovery, I decided to bring her a present. Knowing pack rats are fond of shiny things, I dug in the ground for a shell remnant. When I found a large, luminous pink shell scrap, I cleaned it up and laid it near the foot of the tree branch I'd seen her mount.

On my next visit to the campsite, the shell scrap was gone. I was delighted! You would have thought the Queen of England had deigned to accept my birthday present into the royal collection.

At that time, back in New Jersey, I was meeting with a group at church that discussed deepening our spirituality. Before I returned to California again (to care for my ailing parents), I gave the group an assignment: for our next meeting, find a shiny present for a pack rat. I explained about my little friend and sent them forth.

"No fair getting a dime out of your purse," I said. "You have to find something on the ground or sidewalk for it to count."

At the next meeting, everyone brought something shiny to contribute, from gum wrappers to a clear ballpoint-pen cap. They remarked that the game of searching for something shiny helped them, indeed, find meaning in everyday places. So off I went to California with my little load of presents.

When David and I made our way to the campsite again, I laid out our offerings underneath the bay tree with great pride. Then I proceeded to set up our usual camp. I spread out a tarp with two sleeping bags on it near the foot of the tree—we never camped with a tent, as it was usually the dry season—and then built a fire pit using rounded stones we found by the creek. David went into the scrub to write in his journal before gathering firewood and cooking our evening meal.

We spent a contented evening tending the campfire and recalling past adventures.

The next morning, it was already time to pack up and leave, as my mother's health was not stable. During the night the pack rat had taken no interest in our offerings, which was a small disappointment. I figured, though, she would wait until the coast was clear.

Before long I noticed my rental-car keys were missing. Now, you have the advantage of knowing this is a story about a pack rat. I had the disadvantage of knowing I was often a careless and absent-minded person. I knew I'd put those car keys at the head of my sleeping bag, alongside my glasses, which were still there. Hadn't I? I looked in a dozen other places before telling David the sad news.

David was not surprised or irritated. Nothing bothered him on our camping trips. He went into nature with an open mind and few expectations. He suggested we retrace our steps to where we had left the car the day before. Who knew? Perhaps I had dropped the keys along the way or even left them in the car door.

Back we went, but no joy. By this time, the situation was becoming clear: I had all but invited that pack rat to take my car keys—and taken them, she had.

I shall spare you the details of what came next: how we retraced our steps to the camp, packed up everything, and hiked back to the car to call Hertz at the San Francisco Airport, where I had rented the car the day before—only to find that when you put all your effort into locating a campsite that is Back of the Beyond, you may find it has no cell phone reception. How we hiked until we came upon a ranger who very obligingly drove us to a public phone. How Hertz® miraculously said, "Stay right where you are and we will immediately bring you another set of keys," which is why I will never use another rental car company.

A few months passed before we could return to the campsite. By then I felt a little less enthusiasm about the project. Right off, though, I discovered our little line of objects had hardly been disturbed, which caused me to take a closer look at our campsite.

A few moments' examination was enough to tell the story: tiny bits of pack rat fur were scattered all over the area. A predator had happened on the site.

For a while, there was no sign of a pack rat living there. I'd heard that pack rat middens can survive for tens of thousands of years in the desert, but they're only occupied for a few decades. I wondered, *Has this midden run its course?* But then one day, as I see it, a bright young pack rat happened by, perhaps lured by the sight of a plastic pen cap. He ran up the trunk to the midden, looked around, and decided to settle down.

On my last visit, a large family was in residence. Long may they flourish.

It's your turn now

Further thoughts for readers, writers, and storytellers

If you are like me, you often misplace your keys or other important objects. Compose a story about the missing item.

30: Night of the Take-out Eggplant

Each time David Schooley and I went camping in the wilds of northern California, we encountered a new and surprising wild creature. On the last day of one trip, we spent an hour coaxing a reluctant underwater crayfish, sheltered under a rock near the stream's edge, to eat a Thompson Seedless grape. When the crayfish finally scarfed it down, I counted it as a great triumph. But that's not what made the outing so memorable.

A bottle of wine, a very pleasant dinner, and a delightful fire made that evening pass cheerfully. At bedtime we were left with eggplant in a Chinese takeout container. Emboldened by our success with the crayfish, David proposed we leave the Chinese eggplant out and observe what animals approached it during the night.

I should have had the sense to put the kibosh on this proposal. But David was the expert, and I've had the times of my life following his lead. So we bedded down by the low light of the remaining campfire and waited. As usual, I fell asleep in no time.

I woke in the middle of the night when David nudged me. Two skunks faced off over the eggplant. One was a standard black-and-white-striped skunk, which, from my vantage point on the ground six or eight feet away, was the size of a warship. The other was a smaller, squirrel-sized variety I had never seen before—tan with white spots. Both held their tails erect.

As I lay in my sleeping bag, I wondered what to do next. I decided to do as David was doing: exactly nothing. I went back to sleep. The next time I woke up, the crisis had been resolved. The black-and-white skunk had taken sole possession of the Chinese eggplant.

The rest of the night seemed to pass uneventfully. The next morning, we carefully packed up, removed all traces of our camp, and departed.

David is a man of few words, so he didn't mention what occurred as I slept. Every now and then, while reminiscing, one of us said, "Remember the two skunks and the Chinese eggplant?" Then we chuckled and changed the subject.

So some time passed before I heard the rest of the story. Finally, one day about ten years later, David said, "You certainly were amazing the night we fed the Chinese eggplant to the skunks."

I was puzzled.

"Amazing? I didn't do much except sleep through most of it."

"Surely you couldn't have slept through *everything*."

"Since I was asleep at the time, I have no idea what you mean by *everything*. What did I miss?"

"After the skunk standoff had lasted awhile, the big skunk chased the little one away. You and I must have laid our bedrolls down over an established skunk path." He looked at me hard, as if to catch me pretending I didn't know the rest of the story. But I was clueless.

"When the skunks left our campground, they ran straight at us—no, straight *over* us, with the large skunk chasing the smaller one. Without paying us any attention at all, they ran up your sleeping bag and right under your nose before running over *my* chest and out into the night. Whew! Those skunks really stank! For all these years I've been admiring you for staying stock-still through it all, and then never even mentioning it afterwards. Now it seems you were asleep. You always said you were a sound sleeper, but you set some sort of record that night."

When I look back at this encounter, I can't say I had any sort of meaningful interaction with the skunks. Although they left a big impression on me, basically they came, ate our eggplant, and left, totally ignoring us the whole time.

Perhaps, with wild skunks, this is about the best you can ask for.

It's your turn now

Further thoughts for readers, writers, and storytellers

Some people can sleep through anything. Can you remember a time when you, or the person you were with, slept through a major incident?

31: Cougar Watches

Cougars are patient. They watch, they learn, they bide their time.

I was backpacking in a wild area of northern California scrub country with David Schooley when we approached what was to be our campsite. David looked in all directions to make sure no one was nearby, and then slipped between two bushes and out of sight. A few moments later he was back, declared the coast clear, and summoned me in.

"I've camped here before. It's an ideal place for a campsite," he said, "except for the lack of a water source, which is why we had to backpack in three days' supply of water."

I saw a thirty-foot circular clearing with a concrete slab toward the middle—an artifact left by some long-ago person whose intent we could only guess. The clearing was encircled by heavy brush.

"You see?" David declared, clearly satisfied. "The slab will be perfect to build a campfire, and the dense brush will keep the fire from being seen."

I was not immediately enthusiastic.

"Do you see those holes in the brush?"

I pointed to several tunnels made through the thick foliage by animals entering and leaving our proposed campsite.

"What made those holes?" I asked.

David looked for a moment.

"Oh, those would be cougar holes," he said, dismissively. "No other animal is tall enough to leave such a high tunnel through the brush. A bobcat's would be much shorter."

"You're telling me we're going to camp in a mountain lion's lair?" I protested.

"Yes. They will not bother us. They are really rather shy. If you meet one, don't run away from them, of course."

Whenever we went camping, David always seemed to know best, so that was that. We set up our campsite, gathered firewood, built our fire, had dinner, and spent a pleasant evening around the campfire.

In the morning, David, a light sleeper, reported that during the night a cougar had slunk into the clearing. When he sat bolt upright in his sleeping bag, he said, the cougar leapt into the air, did a 180-degree turn, and left in a flash. I slept through the incident.

On our second day we hiked and swam in a lake about a mile from our campsite, which, along with the routines of camp tending, occupied the day very happily.

When camping in the wild, each of us made a small latrine for ourselves a short distance from the campsite. We dug a good hole with a stick and covered it with dirt after use. After my swim I went to my spot only to discover it was no longer private. A cougar had discreetly left his calling card directly on top of mine. The message could not have been clearer: this was his territory, and he would appreciate it very much if we would clear out.

I began to think that would be a very good idea.

I reported this communication to David, who was not overly impressed, but agreed it was probably just as well we were leaving the next day. Still, today is today, he said, and it was time to gather wood for our evening campfire. We split up in our search. Soon I was gathering three-foot lengths of dry wood and stashing them under each arm.

Loaded up, I walked down a narrow trail not far from camp. A low sound emanated from the brush. At first I thought I was making this noise with my firewood, because it was perfectly coordinated with every step I took. But four such sounds were all I needed to realize they were grunts, large-animal grunts, cougar grunts.

I stopped in my tracks and peered into the brush in front of me, not moving a muscle. There, staring directly at me, not more than five feet away and framed by bushes, was the face of a cougar.

In the minute that followed, several thoughts raced through my head. Most of all, I thought about what those grunts meant. They were certainly not threatening growls, I told myself, but simply warnings—*"Keep your distance, Lady."* Well, I certainly wasn't going to get any closer, so that should be OK.

For a long moment we looked at each other. I was struck by the beauty of the cougar's head. From the corner of each eye, a dark line flowed down each side of the nose as if great black tears had been shed. I envisioned his face sculpted in gold and faience by one of King Tut's great artists.

The power of his gaze arrested me. This was no alien being, but a fellow walker on the Earth. In that moment I felt a deep connection.

But that moment could not last. The pounding of my heart reminded me the cougar could change in an instant. Just in case, I hastily reviewed what I knew about facing a cougar. Stand your ground, the rules went, and try to make yourself look larger than you are. *How to make myself look larger? Hmm. I could raise my arms above my head.* So I did that.

I did not anticipate that my large armloads of firewood would immediately clatter to the ground, making a dreadful racket. Abruptly, the cougar vanished into the brush.

We would not see him again. But he had made his point well enough: it was time for us to go.

The next morning we packed up, cleaned the campsite thoroughly, and left.

That cougar had spoken to me in a way I cannot forget. As we looked so intimately at each other, I felt the force of his intelligence. He showed me, in the firmest but most delicate way he knew, that I was a trespasser on his land, a trespasser against whom he somehow knew his beauty and power were ultimately unavailing. I can still see what I saw as he looked at me— the great black tears falling from his eyes.

It's your turn now

Further thoughts for readers, writers, and storytellers

Perhaps you can recall coming unexpectedly upon a wild animal—one that impressed you deeply. Why not write about that encounter? If you had it to do over again, would you react differently? Did something change for you?

VI: Crossing Paths

32: What Does a Goldfish Want?

For the most part, people go by too quickly to find out what they're all about. That's frustrating for a people-lover like me. But sometimes a window opens abruptly into another's life, and you connect in a special way, if only for a golden moment.

So it was, one day in Manhattan. My husband and I caught a taxi going downtown. The driver was, of course, facing away from us, but we saw his name and a pleasant photograph of a large-eyed man with salt-and-pepper hair on the license he displayed.

Stefan, who is interested in names, started a conversation.

"Where are you from?" he asked.

"Oh, so you noticed my name," the driver replied. "I live in the Bronx, but originally I came from Poland."

"My name, Stefan, sounds Polish, but I'm nothing so colorful. Just an ordinary American."

"No one is ordinary," the driver responded with a chuckle. "Even my goldfish are extraordinary, in their own way."

"How so?" I asked, detecting a good anecdote coming on.

"I've had goldfish for years, and have always liked them, but they do not live very long—two, three years at most, and usually one of them is aggressive and picks on the others until it is the only one left. Not a happy life."

As he talked, he wove his way through the dense traffic with practiced ease.

"But one day when I was starting with a fresh batch of fish, it occurred to me to wonder, *What does a goldfish want?* Then I answered my own question: *Maybe, just maybe, they would like to be touched.* So every night when I came home, after feeding them, I reached into the tank and stroked the water. At first they dodged me, but after a few days they began to get the idea.

"Eventually, they eagerly rose to the surface and darted toward my hand to be petted. I made sure each one got its turn. After a while they made way for each other. I noticed they never attacked one another, as my previous goldfish had done. Seven years after I got them, they are still flourishing."

With those words, he pulled up to our destination.

"What a wonderful story!'" I told him. "I'm sorry to see we have to get out. I'll bet you have other tales to tell."

He laughed.

"Perhaps you will catch my cab another day," he said.

We never saw him again, but I can never forget his words: "No one is ordinary, not even my goldfish."

It's your turn now

Further thoughts for readers, writers, and storytellers

If you make a habit of searching for the extraordinary in humans and other creatures, you will surely find it. Recall an extraordinary encounter you had with someone, perhaps a stranger.

33: Murder and the Christmas Tree Ornament

O ur only child, Jessica, has what used to be called Asperger's syndrome, a high-functioning form of autism spectrum disorder. A specialist seeing her as an adult clinched the diagnosis. We told her of Jessica's fierce obsession with dinosaurs at age three, on top of all her other symptoms.

"That's Asperger's, all right," she said.

As a young child, Jessica could not converse in sentences, but at age three she read and answered questions very well. She even loved to do so on her favorite topics.

So we devised The Dinosaur Game, which involved asking her questions.

"I am a herbivorous dinosaur with a domed head and a beak," we'd say. "Who am I?"

"Pachycephalosaurus!" she roared back, triumphantly.

This game could go on for a half hour or longer. We often played it in restaurants, especially while waiting for our orders to appear—a time when restlessness can get the better of three-year-olds.

One November night at a Chinese restaurant in Parsippany, New Jersey, our game caught the attention of Mr. Sang, the restaurant owner. Seeing this diminutive girl snap out arcane answers to complex questions fascinated him. He pulled up a chair, as if to watch some magical infant tennis match.

He summoned his wife from the back room to watch the "show," which she did with equal fascination.

"She is a miracle child!" he said, finally.

With that, they got up and went back to work.

We were tickled by their appreciation. At the end of the meal, Mr. Sang appeared again, to give Jessica a square, green cloth-covered box, with a padded lid. It opened to reveal a beautiful, embroidered, silken ornament of an abstract design. Its center section looked like stuffed orange segments, beaded in tiny pearls. Emerging from the tip of each segment was an embroidered arc ending in sparkling gold tassels. It was elegant.

Jessica took to it immediately. We thanked the owner warmly. We decided to hang the ornament on our Christmas tree and return to the restaurant often. Perhaps, we mused, the Sangs might be a weekly substitute for Jessica's grandparents, who lived three thousand miles away and couldn't participate in her daily life.

Sadly, we never got the chance to find out. Three days later, the restaurant owner and his wife were brutally murdered by gunmen. They were shot in their driveway as they drove up to their home. We were appalled when we read about it in the newspaper. It seemed there might have been some underworld matter of a debt unpaid, or thought to be unpaid.

We looked to our new ornament for answers, but it twirled and sparkled enigmatically.

We told Jessica our new friends had died unexpectedly and had gone to join the angels. She accepted the story, but for us, sudden death had doused our joy and put a damper on our Christmas revelries that year.

The next year I lifted our Chinese restaurant ornament out of the box when we decorated the tree. I hesitated before hanging it. *Too many sad associations*, I thought. But Jess's face lit up when she saw the colorful orb, and I was glad I had.

It was the beginning of a realization—in a world where bad things happen, we must make room for improbable connections, for things to celebrate. Forty-some years later, the ornament still makes its annual appearance on the tree and we once again somberly yet warmly remember Mr. and Mrs. Sang.

It's your turn now

Further thoughts for readers, writers, and storytellers

Joy and sadness—are they not often mixed in our recollections? Can you bring to mind such a mixture from your own life?

34: Miss Kaloud Changes Everything

During our only child Jessica's second year, she withdrew from most people. Although her vocabulary of individual words grew very large, she didn't progress to speaking in sentences. Moreover, she had increasing trouble understanding what was said to her.

Reading, however, came easily. An instant devotee of *Sesame Street*, then a new television show, she learned all the letters of the alphabet. By the time she was twenty months old, she could read one or two simple words.

I didn't know quite what to make of her strange mixture of strengths and weaknesses.

A dear friend of ours, a clinical social worker dealing with children, told me Jessica treated her essentially the way she would a chair or some other object in the room. She said professionals should see her. So began rounds of visits to a child psychologist, a social worker, and a neurologist. No one had a diagnosis or any concrete help to offer.

By the time Jessica was three, she read with complete fluency and comprehension. Having fallen in love with dinosaurs, she collected lots of plastic ones. She lined them up and played with them. She pored over her many dinosaur books. But if I wanted her attention, I had to reach down and touch her, or lift her face toward mine and speak very slowly and simply, as if she were hard of hearing.

She started speaking in sentences but often with what is called echolalia. If I asked her, "How is your jigsaw puzzle going?" she might answer with the same question, as if I were trying to teach her to say it. There was also a great deal of what professionals call "word salad," meaning her words came out in random order, as if they'd been tossed in the air and landed any which way. Yet if I could not communicate with her by saying something, I could write it down or sing it to her and be perfectly understood. Jessica was a conundrum.

So we added a speech therapist to our group of professional helpers, which is how Miss Kaloud briefly came into our lives. Miss Kaloud, a pretty young woman who worked at the local hospital, clearly gave Jessica her fullest and most thoughtful attention. Jessica seemed to enjoy her first three sessions. So we were happy to persevere even though the progress achieved seemed minute. By the third session, even that modest headway had vanished.

Still, we were hopeful. We had no other choices.

In the meantime Jessica turned four-and-a-half. We faced this question: could she function in a public school kindergarten, or would she need special school placement?

Searching for an answer, we visited a child psychiatrist who had a reputation as an ultimate diagnostician. After interviewing my husband and me twice, he had a session with Jessica, who spent the entire time yelling—not desperate to get out of the room, just yelling. The psychiatrist told us regular public school was not the place for her. Sorrowfully, we scheduled an interview for admission to the special school.

It was time for Jessica's fourth speech therapy appointment. As we walked into Miss Kaloud's office, I noticed that her smile, always welcoming, was particularly bright.

"I think I may have some promising news for you," Miss Kaloud said. "I have just come from a case presentation that reminded me of Jessica. It was about an eight-year-old boy who seems to have just about the same language difficulties and strengths that Jessica has. Three weeks ago, he was put on the drug Ritalin®, and this week he said, 'For the first time in my life, my mind is clear.'"

Encountering that sentence once again after forty-five years still sends a chill down my spine. What a difference it made in our lives. I left that session with Miss Kaloud, called our pediatric neurologist, explained what had happened at the case presentation, and asked if Jessica could take Ritalin®. After some consultation and consideration, the neurologist agreed.

Three weeks later we had our last appointment with Miss Kaloud. After starting the drug, Jessica had absorbed every lesson Miss Kaloud taught her. There would be no more speech therapy sessions. We said a tearful farewell to Miss Kaloud.

The next week we had our interview with the director of the special school. After testing Jessica, the director approached us with a bright smile. Jessica had failed the entrance examination, she said. A public school's Child Study Team could handle her remaining difficulties.

This story is not a promotion for Ritalin®. Every child is different. Few fit the profile of characteristics Jessica presented. I've left out many to keep things simple. The neurologist eventually identified Jessica as "borderline autistic" with Attention Deficit Disorder.

Every year that passed, we took her off Ritalin® for six weeks to see how she managed. The first year, she returned to the echolalic, often-silent child who spoke in word salad. When we put her back on the medication, she returned to "normal."

Every year that followed, when we took her off the drug, she fell less far behind, until finally, at age thirteen, there was no observable difference. So we discontinued the medication for good.

Her teachers and the Child Study Team were a great support to her throughout her school years.

Jessica graduated and went on to a good college and then Princeton University for a master's degree in musicology. She lives independently and supports herself as a proofreader who specializes in editing diverse foreign languages.

After that final session with Miss Kaloud, despite the enormous change she wrought in our lives, we never saw her again. I wanted her to know how well Jessica was doing, but I learned she'd gotten married, changed her name, and moved away. I never got a forwarding address.

If you ever meet a former speech therapist whose maiden name was Kaloud, tell her a family in New Jersey remembers her gratefully.

It's your turn now

Further thoughts for readers, writers, and storytellers

You may once have found yourself in a serious predicament with no apparent way out. Then someone came along and handed you the key to your difficulties. Writing about what happened is one way to express your gratitude.

35: Intruder

An unearthly shriek woke me at 3 a.m. I could have sworn it came from next to my husband's side of the bed, but Stefan was away on a business trip. I was alone in the house. I was acutely aware of my surroundings but paralyzed with fear, imprisoned in my own body, unable to move a muscle.

Rustling noises had accompanied the outburst, but they died down immediately, as if the intruder were aware I was now awake.

Stefan, an untidy mathematician, had left his pile of work papers next to the bedroom door. *An unwary trespasser could easily trip over it and shriek*, I told myself.

As I lay there in the ominous silence that followed, memories flashed through my mind: I'd faced down a cougar with equanimity. I'd slept next to fighting skunks with erect tails. Yet here I was, terror-stricken for the first time. The thought of a burglar or rapist, or even a murderer, in my room—well, apparently that was too much even for me.

My mind worked furiously. *What can I do? Obviously, nothing until this paralysis fades. Then perhaps I can reach for the phone—a mere two feet from my hand—and call 911.* But in that moment the phone was hopelessly out of reach.

I strained to catch any further sound. There was none. The intruder seemed as paralyzed as I was. Well and good. I thought of Stefan and my daughter, Jessica, and my parents, who might soon be without me. My life flashed before me in the darkness of the room: a well-loved childhood, a good marriage with its ups and downs, a happy motherhood. All came down to this moment.

Time passed. There was another small noise—some movement in the room. The intruder had roused from his immobility, but I still could not. I thought again about calling 911. The phone—so near and yet so far!

Then a new thought came. *If I call the police, they will surely come, and they will see how messy my room is.* Right then, it was a true uproar of slovenliness, with papers and clothing strewn everywhere. *If it's all a big mistake, I'll end up mortified. But if I just lie here and let whatever happens, happen, I'll probably be dead—and then I won't have to face some policeman seeing the mess.*

At that moment, as shame and then amusement at my reaction overlaid my fear, I relaxed a bit.

Gradually, time passed. I realized I hadn't heard the intruder in a long time. *Could he have withdrawn? Could I have imagined the whole thing? Surely not.* The noises were too real, too immediate.

Yet somehow the incident seemed to pass. I no longer felt his presence.

I calmed down. The paralysis went away. Eventually, I went back to my customary sound sleep. In the morning I found no trace anyone had entered. It was a mystery.

When Stefan returned from his trip, I told him about that night and ruefully disclosed my decision not to call the police. We had a good laugh over my irrational decision-making process and resolved to clean up the place. Soon we did just that, getting the room to a state suitable for police to see.

A couple of weeks passed. One night, as Stefan and I got ready for bed, I heard it again—the shriek that had terrorized me. With the lights on and both of us awake, it was clear the noise came from the attic directly over our heads.

Stefan sprinted for the door to the attic, ran up the stairs two at a time, and came face-to-face with the erstwhile "murderer"—a raccoon, suitably decked out in his burglar's mask, shrinking in a corner. As my husband poked around, I realized the rustling in the attic sounded exactly as if it had come from the bedroom itself.

Stefan shut the attic door firmly. We went to bed.

In the morning we heard no further sounds from above, so Stefan went up to inspect the attic. He soon discovered the raccoon's entry point. A single shingle had been torn off the cedar shake roof. The intruder had a very small head for a raccoon, he said, which probably had enabled him to squeeze through that small space. Thankfully, the raccoon was gone.

We called a roofer to replace the missing shingle. Since no one could come right away, we had a pest control expert set a have-a-heart trap to lure our itinerant visitor.

The exterminator explained it was probably a male raccoon. Female raccoons come in to nest and don't go away, but males move around nightly from one selected site to another, circling back to earlier sites regularly.

"Expect it to return soon," he said.

We baited a Have-a-Heart trap with peanut butter and a dish of water and waited. Sure enough, ten days later the raccoon returned and was trapped. The pest control man took him away, promising to take him to a distant spot from which he'd be unable to find us again.

The affair of the night intruder was over—except for one small footnote. Over the next few weeks I spotted at least two neighbors, owners of cedar-shake-roofed houses, up on their roofs, hammering back shingles. Since they were out of earshot, I didn't ask what had caused their problems, but I was sure I knew.

The raccoon had discovered an easy trick for gaining entry to those cozy-looking houses. He had encircled the neighborhood with his night-time hiding places.

I was glad the pest control man had agreed to release the raccoon in woods—someplace with no shake roofs anywhere nearby.

It's your turn now

Further thoughts for readers, writers, and storytellers

Can you recall a time you were frightened out of your wits? Write about it—get it all out.

36: The Power of Fellowship

A landscape gardener, a social worker, a research scientist, an ICU nurse—encounters with such fellow-congregants at the Morristown (NJ) Unitarian Fellowship over 50 years have given deep meaning to my life. Oh, yes, I've had great friendships there as well--but a friendship is not an encounter, which is a sudden, often unexpected, often life-changing meeting, usually with someone I don't know well, that can jolt me into new awareness.

My Fellowship encounters typically involve what we call "participatory services." These services are presented Sunday mornings by lay members of the congregation, each speaking from personal experience on a topic chosen by a leader.

Limited to four or five minutes each, participants write out their words in advance and get feedback from other members of the group. They become very successful in, say, describing their own spiritual journeys or telling personal accounts that express our shared values.

For years these services have helped me break through habits of mind. Stereotyping is one such habit. It comes too easily—"the old man who walks with a cane," "the woman who dresses so beautifully." Stereotypes keep me, and all of us, from truly encountering another being and finding the amazing realities within.

In 1976, the bicentennial year, I led "Leaves from the American Family Tree," the first participatory service. We retold the history of America through our family stories, ranging from an ancestress who reportedly threw herself overboard from the *Mayflower* to a congregant's own arrival as a recent immigrant.

One participant was Ann Renz, a quiet woman who like me was a displaced native San Franciscan.

"I had an ancestor named the Reverend Ebenezer Devotion, who lived in Massachusetts in the late seventeenth century," she said. "When he died, the newspaper said that his life had been 'the model of all Christian virtues.' His will, which still exists, listed his worldly possessions."

She named several objects—riding boots, say, and a pewter plate—and ended with "Ralph, the Negro man."

Then she sat down, after just thirty seconds.

I was amazed. I wouldn't have been so succinct. And I would have been wrong. I had long thought people who had a lot to say were more interesting than those who didn't. But Ann changed my mind, saying exactly what needed to be said and not a word more.

That small story's full significance played out over the next few years. Our minister wanted a committee to find new ways our congregation could welcome black people. Ann volunteered enthusiastically. Knowing about her slave-owning ancestor deepened my understanding of her commitment to integrating the Fellowship more fully. Though Ann's brief talk contained barely a word about herself, it had taught me much about what she valued. But my deepest lesson from Ann was that people of few words may have great things to say.

Another early participant was Dennis Harvey. Soon after this Englishman immigrated at age thirty-seven with his young family, an overwhelming stroke paralyzed him and took away his vision, memory, and ability to speak. He later recounted to the Fellowship his arduous, piece-by-piece recovery over several Sunday mornings.

In a service called "Turning Points," he described the dramatic moment he recovered language. His paralysis was healed, but despite regular speech therapy, he'd made no progress in talking at all. Not a single word could he utter. One day, the therapist showed him pictures of animals, hoping to prompt a "dog" or "cat." No success. When his session ended, Dennis got up and left the room. In the corridor something came to him. He returned to the therapist's office, poked his head through the doorway, and triumphantly said, "Hippopotamus!"

From then on, he rapidly regained his verbal abilities. Formerly an insurance agent, now a landscape gardener, Dennis always told his stories with humility, self-reflective humor, and enormous gratitude for what had been given back and what he'd learned. Lost in admiration for how Dennis had persevered, for the complexities of the human mind and the resilience of the human spirit, I eventually realized I, too, might possess this potential for overcoming. He inspired many of us.

Sharing experiences in these services can be equally dramatic for the participants. One relative newcomer, George S., described his childhood anguish, growing up as the lone white sheep in a family of career criminals.

"I remember," he said, "how we sat around the kitchen table on Saturday nights, stuffing envelopes with bribes for the local policemen." He vowed to make an honest living, and he did. He became a research scientist at nearby Allied Chemical.

As I listened, I thought of the enduring values that marked my own childhood and marveled at George's drive to break away from morals he didn't share. I was awed by his courage and persistence.

Weeks later, he told me that Sunday morning had changed him. "I always kept my past a dark secret, feeling so ashamed," he said, "but people have been so warm and responsive since I gave my talk. I feel I have begun a new life."

One vivid Fellowship encounter happened not at a service but at a winter solstice concert of Olympia's Daughters, a local women's singing group. It was just before Christmas, but I was not in the holiday mood.

I'd recently returned from a long stint looking after my elderly parents in California. My mother, who had been an invalid for almost a quarter-century, was nearing the end of her life—she would die two months later—and my father was slowly succumbing to the ravages of dementia. It wasn't easy to be away from them at Christmastime. I knew they'd be with friends but not with family. So I had trouble rejoicing over "new life coming to inspire the world," the meaning I usually find in the Christmas story.

But as I slumped in my chair and listened to such carols as "In the Bleak Midwinter" and "Lo, How a Rose E'er Blooming," I let go of my deep sadness. Because I didn't know most of the women, I was drawn to one I knew slightly. Beth Hayward has a lovely, warm, open face at any time, but that day she seemed truly inspired. The melodies flowed through her.

While I listened, I thought of "Grief," a recent participatory Sunday service in which Beth had spoken of her years as an intensive care nurse. Seeing many people approach death, and many grieving families, she had come to understand what they needed from her. She saw it as her great privilege to be present for them. Listening to her soothing, gentle Scottish burr, I imagined the comfort she brought.

Now, hearing her sing with Olympia's Daughters, I felt that solace flowing into my own tattered psyche. I thought of the story of the angel who brought "tidings of great joy" to the Virgin Mary.

They sang "Deep Peace," a song composed by their leader, Penny Gneisen: "Deep peace of the stars that sparkle above, O may they shine their light on you." As she sang, Beth seemed to bring those words to life.

I received that benediction in the darkest corners of my tired soul. I left the concert ready to go out into the world once more, to do the work given me to do in the lives of those dear to me.

It's your turn now

Further thoughts for readers, writers, and storytellers

People you know slightly may be as rich in meaning as presents under the Christmas tree. The more you open yourself to learning about them, the more your life—and your own story—may be enhanced. Observe, rejoice, create.

37: Billy Jamieson and the Saga of the Seal Stone

M y mother and I first came upon the seal stone around 1960 in a California antique store. We'd been prowling for whatever we could find when, between a ladies' writing desk and a Victorian whatnot, we saw a 2½' x 3' volcanic stone, apparently basalt, weighing more than 250 pounds, and carved all over with strange symbols.

The dealer said it had been engraved in prehistoric times and came from a small island near Attu, off Alaska near the tip of the Aleutian Island chain. A serviceman stationed at an air base there had found it. When he flew to the San Francisco Bay Area, he brought the stone along and tried to sell it for a lot of money. But he ran out of time and had to virtually give it away to the dealer, who offered it to us for twenty-five dollars. Careful not to show our delight, we said, "Sure." Then we carted it home. My father created a proud place for it in the Japanese garden he'd designed and built in our yard in Berkeley.

When we studied the stone carefully, we made out eyes, nostrils, and a mouth, a fin or flipper on one side, and notches at the base that could represent flipper tips. Many more abstract designs covered the flat back of the stone. At first we thought it represented a fish. But because of the nostrils on the top, we decided it depicted a mammal. Then, because of the many circles on the stone, we deemed it a ringed seal, the sort that swims in those latitudes. From then on, we called it the seal stone.

Later, when my parents moved to nearby Orinda, my father made another Japanese garden and placed the seal stone there. It even went along to their final home in Walnut Creek, where it dominated their small terrace.

My family didn't feel at all awkward about having this exotic prehistoric stone. In my childhood we had once seen Indian engravings on rocks outside Fallon, Nevada. Someone had located the local dump on top of the petroglyphs. To see the carvings, we had to scrape wilted lettuce and other debris off the rocks. In the case of the seal stone, we felt we were caring for something precious that otherwise might have been destroyed. Turned out later, we were right.

When my parents died and I inherited the seal stone, I wanted to authenticate it and find it a proper home where it would be appreciated. Maybe a museum somewhere would be interested in purchasing it. I didn't want to move it to the East Coast, where I lived. It could break in transit. My brother-in-law, Larry Burr, agreed to take it to his Marin County home, where it remained for about ten years. At that time I gave him half-ownership of the stone. He somehow pinpointed the name of the place from which it was most likely taken, Shemya Island., site of an American air base in the post-war years.

In 2010 Larry, a professional photographer (among other interesting things), took a good picture I sent to experts who could authenticate the seal stone. After many false starts and people who called it a fake, a friend's son suggested we contact Billy Jamieson, a Canadian tribal-arts dealer in Toronto.

Billy turned out to be one of the most interesting people I've ever encountered—not just one of Canada's premier tribal-arts dealers, but a unique combination of P. T. Barnum and Indiana Jones. He was the catalyst in finding the seal stone's true home and getting it the scientific recognition it deserved.

Our first contacts with Billy were over the Internet. We got off on the wrong foot when he said that, although the picture was interesting, he thought it was a recent soapstone carving by Eskimo artisans. I protested.

"The stone would be an impractical fake," I said. "It's a very hard volcanic rock that would have taken ages to carve."

"I don't think it's authentic," he replied, "but I'll give you $700 for the stone. I'd like to have it as a garden ornament."

I was miffed. The stone already had spent several decades of its life as a garden ornament. I had higher aspirations for it. I refused to sell.

"We're looking for a buyer who recognizes it for what it is—a prehistoric Aleut carved stone," I said.

Billy hesitated.

"All right, I'll send the photo to some experts I know," he said. "I'll be in touch next week."

As it happened, I told him, I'd be in Toronto, where he lived, that week. He could phone me at my hotel. I'd never been to Toronto. It was pure coincidence that my husband, Stefan, and I had planned a trip there with some old friends.

Halfway through our stay, Billy called to say he'd heard from the experts. They believed it was authentic. They also agreed with Larry that the stone probably came from Shemya Island, a rocky, wind-scarred little island where the U.S. air base had displaced the original inhabitants.

The experts, who were from the University of Alaska's Museum of the North in Fairbanks, were excited to hear about the stone and were, as Billy expressed it, "turning cartwheels for joy over the discovery." Nothing like the seal stone had ever been found in the Aleutians, although the resemblance to shapes in later antler and bone artifacts found on the island pointed to its authenticity.

"Yes, experts agree that it is the real thing, impossibly rare and important to the history of that area. That's the good news," Billy said, "but there is some bad news as well: it doesn't belong to you!"

"How can that be? My family has owned it for decades."

"I was told it is the property of the federal government. By law and by treaty, everything in the Aleutian Islands belongs to the Feds, including everything removed from there."

"So we are obliged to give it back?"

"Yes. Due to an agreement between the museum and the U.S. Fish and Wildlife Service, which administers the law, the stone will probably come to rest at that very museum.

"I would like to help you return this stone to Alaska," Billy added. "Why don't you come over to my place so we can talk about it?"

Soon Stefan and I found ourselves entering the most amazing home we had seen in our lives or are ever likely to see.

We took an elevator to the second floor. It opened into a darkened but dramatically lit marble-floored circular foyer. Against the wall opposite us stood a figure dressed in a straw medicine man's costume and mask. On the near wall hung a skeletal figure woven of rattan and decorated with a skull mask. The pillar in the center of the room was an old Northwest totem pole.

Before I could take in the rest of the figures that lined the room, Jamieson appeared and welcomed us. He greeted us warmly and offered to show us around. Jamieson cut an impressive figure, tall with long black hair and a face leathered by many sunbaked days doing archaeological fieldwork in Ecuador, Peru, New Guinea, and other remote climes. Skittering along after him was his little dachshund, Ramses.

The dog, it turned out, was named for the pharaoh Ramses I, whose 3,300-year-old mummy Billy had acquired when he purchased the contents of the Niagara Falls Museum. In the sale he'd also gotten two-headed calves, nine unidentified Egyptian mummies, and Wild Bill Hickok's saddle. Many of the home's objects, we learned, came from the museum's collections, amassed during the late nineteenth and early twentieth centuries by the intrepid explorers of that era.

After one mummy was examined and pronounced to be that of Ramses I, Billy had sold it to the Egyptian government for $2,000,000.

Billy had unearthed, bought, or traded many other items. As he told us, gatherings of the U.S. and Canadian branches of the Explorer's Club often met in his home. I imagine they would consider it a dream of a setting for their deliberations.

As we toured the three-story home, he introduced us to many wonders. Billy's tastes in collecting were oriented toward the bizarre. I counted at least a dozen shrunken heads and a number of skulls ornamented with carved and even bejeweled designs. One item was an oak electric chair, taken from a New York state prison, which had been designed by Gustav Stickley himself. It exhibited all the features of a genuine antique Stickley armchair, complete with its metal stamped label.

In his den was the intricately carved wooden model of the submarine Nautilus that had been used in the Disney movie 20,000 *Leagues under the Sea.* On a high bookshelf we saw a lifelike wax head—a likeness, Billy said, of Monsieur Gustave Eiffel, of Eiffel Tower fame, from Madame Tussaud's personal collection.

Descending into the basement via an elegant Art Deco staircase, we saw collections of tribal war clubs, butterflies, and stuffed animal heads lining the deep red walls. Later, on a second-floor landing, we came upon a wooden crate in front of a sofa.

"Is that crate an article of furniture or something more?" Stefan asked.

"It just arrived yesterday," Billy said. "Would you like to see what is in it?"

"Yes!" Stefan said.

Billy pulled aside the crate's cover to reveal an Egyptian mummy case.

"The contents are intact, I assure you," he said. "They're just waiting to be carbon dated."

The rear end of an antique horse-and-buggy hearse, complete with a saltwater fish tank, projected from one wall. It was said to be haunted.

"With all the remnants of other lives surrounding you, it must be hard for you to sleep at night," I said.

Billy laughed.

"No, my nights are untroubled."

As we marveled over one amazing article after another, I asked Billy how he had gotten started in this business.

"I began as an aluminum-siding contractor with an interest in archaeology and fantastical curiosities," he said. "A trip through the Amazon River Basin convinced me to pursue the life of an amateur archaeologist, dealer, and collector. So I began selling what I collected on my travels."

Billy planned to produce a television series on interesting artifacts from around the world. He said he'd like to film an episode that included the story of our seal stone, its origins in the Aleutian Islands, its discovery by the U.S. airman who brought it to California, its purchase for $25, and its subsequent ownership by my family. He would come to our house in New Jersey, film us talking about the stone, go to California to film the stone being packed for its trip to Alaska, and then finally film it in its new home at the Museum of the North.

He offered to pay for shipping the stone to Alaska, a packing job that would require an expert in shipping heavy art objects.

Moreover, Billy proposed to pay us $3,000, which would go to Larry, for all his efforts. My visit with Billy had completely won me over. I was really pleased that the stone would land in a research museum with the where-withal to uncover its origin and perhaps determine its age.

We had to discuss the matter with Stefan's brother, Larry, the half-owner of the stone. Then we took our leave of the astonishing place and the man whose vision had created it.

Larry did not like the idea of giving the stone back to the federal government. He wanted to fight for ownership, or at least compensation, in court. I thought it unlikely we would win and that we'd probably spend more to contest the matter than we could recover.

Eventually, Larry gave in. The TV crew came to our home and filmed an interview. Soon after, the stone was crated up in California under the camera's watchful eye and shipped off to Fairbanks, where its arrival and uncrating made a satisfying stir. Having it returned to its native Alaska after more than half a century was a great relief and joy to me.

Ironically, if the stone had been left on the island, it probably would've been destroyed when the air base was built. No artifacts seem to have remained above ground after the military construction was completed. So the airman who illegally removed the stone in the first place had done it a favor.

Stefan and I traveled to Alaska to see the seal stone at the Museum of the North, where it was being studied. We were shown the spot where the stone was to be exhibited—in a hall that contains samples of the best art from the entire history of Alaska to the present day, including oil paintings and sculptures. We were told the seal stone would have a place of honor as the oldest object on display there—a great distinction.

I like to think that Aleuts, descendants of those who carved the stone, may one day see it there and realize their ancestors were not just ingenious survivors but also artists and meaning-makers, dreamers of a great dream we can only wonder at.

Billy Jamieson went on to film a number of segments for his TV show, slated to premiere on the Canadian History Channel in the fall of 2011 and, if all went well, in the United States the following year. But life is not predictable. In July 2011 Billy Jamieson died suddenly, unexpectedly, at home on his fifty-seventh birthday. Plans for his TV show had to be abbreviated. Only eight episodes were filmed. As the stone had not yet been enshrined in its ultimate location at the time of Billy's death, the seal stone episode remained uncompleted--hence no $3,000 for Larry.

Still, the film that was aired stands as a tribute to Billy. He was one of a kind, a truly amazing man. Without him, the seal stone might never have found its way home to Alaska.

It's your turn now

Further thoughts for readers, writers, and storytellers

Maybe you have objects with a long story that are very precious to you. Pass along their stories so others may come to understand how meaningful are your treasures. Make us see and feel their significance.

VII: Touching History

38: The FBI Comes Calling

L et me acknowledge it right off—when I was young, I, um, fibbed to the FBI. Not once, but twice.

When I first encountered an FBI man, I was eleven years old, leaning out of an upstairs window, wrapped body and head in towels. I'd just gotten out of the shower when the doorbell rang. This was 1952, a time we trusted most people around us. But I did not trust the FBI.

The FBI agent, neatly dressed in a suitably sober suit and craning his head back, flashed his badge at me.

"I wonder, since there is no adult home to speak to, if I could ask you a few questions?"

"Sure," I said.

I was ready for him. My father had taken me aside one day and said, in serious tones that made me pay careful attention, "You know, Betsy, we have a lot of friends whose work may attract the interest of the government."

I knew all about Senator Joseph McCarthy, the House Un-American Activities Committee, and the atmosphere of fear they had aroused, nationally and among some of my parents' friends. And I knew that J. Edgar Hoover's FBI was part of that fearsome movement. I was a flaming opponent.

"Someone from the FBI may come to the door some day and ask you questions about one of our friends," my father continued. "If they ask you what we talk about in our home, you just tell them, 'Literature, art, and music.' Nothing about politics."

In the 1940s and '50s, I was growing up in Berkeley, California, surely one of the most interesting places for a family attuned to the currents moving through American society. My father was a civil engineer responsible for bringing water resources to the eastern half of the San Francisco Bay Area, but he was interested in many other things, too. My mother was a former English teacher, presently working at the university, and my father's mother, who lived with us, was a retired concert singer and voice teacher.

Our family's varied interests were reflected in our friends, who included a seismologist, a geophysicist, a historian, musicians, artists, a music and art critic for the *San Francisco Chronicle*, a mathematician, a philosopher, and a CEO, who lived across the street from us. As an only child, I was always included in their frequent gatherings. I listened hard, and my opinions were often solicited, which probably helped give me an artificial-seeming grown-up air.

It turned out the FBI man was interested in the CEO, who was up for appointment as head of a sensitive international organization. Now, as it happened, I knew something about this man that I thought the FBI might want to know—namely, that he drank a *lot*. And my mother had told me she had seen him being carried home, feet first, at 3 one morning. But that was hearsay, wasn't it? And who would take a child's word for it? Anyway, I was determined to give away nothing.

Finally, the FBI man got around to the Question: "What do people talk about when they gather in your home?"

And I knew just what to say. With a nonchalant toss of my toweled head, I replied, "Oh, literature, art, and music"—which was true, up to a point. Political discussions were frequent, with the CEO, for example, defending Eisenhower against an array of Democrats. But I wondered, *Surely it wasn't against the law to be liberal Democrats—or was it?*

With this, the interview drew speedily to an end. I was quite proud of myself, and I repeated the gist of my interview with some glee to my parents when they returned.

Whatever the FBI made of this interview, the CEO received his appointment without a hitch and served his term without apparent trouble.

Time passed—ten years, actually—before I heard from the FBI again. At that point I had graduated from college and was back home in the Berkeley house, getting ready for graduate school. The phone rang. An FBI man explained he wanted to interview me about a close friend and fellow graduate taking a job in the aerospace industry. My friend needed a security clearance. I agreed to meet him at a café on the campus, where I was taking a course.

"How will I recognize you?" he asked.

I thought I would have a little fun with the FBI man.

"I will be wearing a rose in my buttonhole."

We met up successfully. My new FBI man looked much the same as my old one, dressed in the same type of cookie-cutter suit, which added a bit to my sense of superiority. He asked me questions that had no difficult overtones, as my friend from college was as much a straight arrow as the FBI could wish for. But then came the famous Question.

"When you and your friend get together, what do you like to talk about?"

I could not resist.

"Oh, literature, art, and music," I said with an echo of my old nonchalance.

Whereupon the FBI man stopped taking notes, put down his notebook, and looked at me keenly.

"I think I know you," he said. "I interviewed you ten years ago at your home. You leaned out of an upstairs window with a towel wrapped around your head and answered some questions for me then."

I was flummoxed. It had not occurred to me that my answer, which I had thought so clever, was too clever by half for an eleven-year-old girl and might stick in the mind of an FBI man as readily as it had stuck in my own.

It has entered my mind since the passage of the Freedom of Information Act to write and see whether my smart-aleck remark had garnered me a place in the annals of the FBI, but I have decided not to. If the answer were Yes, it would be too disturbing, and if the answer were No, too disappointing.

It's your turn now

Further thoughts for readers, writers, and storytellers

Did you know a family secret in your childhood that you were never, ever supposed to let outsiders find out about? Were you ever prodded to disclose it? There's a story waiting to be told.

39: Endurance

I was born just months before Pearl Harbor. Nevertheless, my early life was relatively untouched by World War II.

My father, having been rejected by the armed services for poor teeth and bad eyesight, worked during the war for Boeing Aircraft in Seattle. He designed fire-extinguishing systems for the B-29 bomber and other planes.

I helped my father tend our Victory Garden and helped my mother lower the blackout blinds each night. Other than those activities, the war didn't intrude into what were happy years for me.

As I grew older, though, I learned what others close to me had experienced during the war. The lives of my two best friends in grammar school had been radically affected. May's Jewish family was fortunate to get the last boat out of Nazi Germany in 1939. Ann's family was imprisoned by the Japanese in a Philippine concentration camp, barely escaping with their lives when American troops liberated them in 1945.

In junior high, I had a close Jewish friend, Marion, whose family had fled Nazi persecution in Czechoslovakia. Kurt, a Jewish friend of my family, had fled Austria with his own family for the Far East, ending up in Shanghai.

A college roommate, Keiko, was an American-born citizen of Japanese ancestry who spent the war years in an American "concentration camp" in Washington State—not far from where I lived during those years, but under very different circumstances.

So growing up, I was exposed to many different life stories of the war, all with a common theme: children stuck in circumstances beyond their control who had endured much and grew to maturity in 1950s America. I have lost track of Marion and Ann, but I know the others went on to lead successful lives. Their pain and resilience have lived with me down the years. I carry them with me like a beautiful patchwork quilt, sometimes a burden but more often a source of inspiration.

Some war stories came to me through my mother. When I was a teenager, she told me about something that had happened in 1946. She had been a high school English teacher in Lodi, California. So had her best friend, Esther Ingerson. One day after classes were over, a young uniformed soldier came to Mrs. Ingerson's classroom. He reminded her of his name. He had been a student of hers before the war. She remembered him but was surprised to see him. He had not been a particularly eager student.

"I want to thank you," he said, "for saving my life." She was puzzled, but he went on.

"You once assigned a poem for us to memorize. I did so, somewhat reluctantly—frankly, it was a bit over my head at that age. But later on, it came back to me as the most important set of words I had ever heard. You see, it rescued me during the Bataan Death March."

Mrs. Ingerson would have known about that infamous event in 1942: the Japanese forced thousands of prisoners to walk sixty miles through nearly impenetrable jungles, having almost nothing to eat. Of the approximately seventy-five thousand men who started, ten thousand died during the march.

"How did you make it through?" she asked.

"I recited to myself that poem at every turn, willing myself to go on, as the author had. It gave me the strength to endure the unendurable."

Mrs. Ingerson was very touched. She asked him to recite the poem for her, and he did, through eyes bright with tears.

Invictus

by William Ernest Henley

Out of the night that covers me,
Black as the pit from pole to pole,

I thank whatever gods may be
For my unconquerable soul.

In the fell clutch of circumstance
I have not winced, or cried aloud.
Under the bludgeonings of chance
My head is bloodied, but unbowed.

Beyond this place of wrath and tears
Looms but the horrors of the shade,
And yet the menace of the years
Finds and shall find me unafraid.

It matters not how strait the gate,
How charged with punishments the scroll,
I am the master of my fate,
I am the captain of my soul.

This story touched me enormously, becoming an important part of my understanding of the war. It taught me that the words we carry with us can profoundly affect our lives in ways we cannot anticipate.

Years later, it influenced my decision to major in English literature, with a special love of poetry.

It's your turn now

Further thoughts for readers, writers, and storytellers

Are there words you have memorized that have come back to rescue you at a crucial moment? What do they mean to you now?

40: Meeting the Campaigners

When I was eleven, I was bitten by the political bug. I don't know how else to describe it. I read a lot of narratives—dog, horse, and Indian stories, historical novels, comic books. But I was not much concerned with the world of politics until the House Un-American Activities Committee reared its ugly head.

My mother told me that people my family knew were suffering because of political views they'd held many years before. Some were threatened at their jobs because they, on principle, refused to sign oaths pledging loyalty to the Constitution and the U.S. government.

My notion that we lived in a free society was shaken to the core. Suddenly, I wanted to become involved.

In 1952, a presidential election year, the Democratic candidate, Governor Adlai Stevenson of Illinois, ran against the Republican candidate, World War II five-star general Dwight Eisenhower. My parents were thinking about voting Democratic, so they bought a book of Adlai Stevenson's collected speeches. I read it with a growing sense of excitement. All the notions I'd been carrying in my head were spelled out there in elegant and thoughtful prose, along with many others that were new to me but lined up with my ideals. I was hooked.

I wanted to see this man for myself, so I persuaded my parents to take me to one of his rallies in San Francisco. I wasn't impressed by the large, excited mass of people. Such crowds reminded me of Hitler's cheering multitudes, which my sixth-grade classmates and I had seen in a movie. I wondered, *How could thinking people be deluded by such crazy ideas?* I concluded the psychological effect of being swept up in a gigantic rally must have something to do with it. I told myself, *Keep your wits about you when you find yourself in such a situation. Remember your own principles, and ask, Do these ideas make sense?* (Yes, I really thought like this at the age of eleven. I didn't even enjoy watching a football game in a stadium when the crowd went wild.)

This being said, when Stevenson spoke, I was smitten. He was not a handsome man. This was a pre-JFK era when political candidates tended to be, from my youthful point of view, baggy old men. When I got close to him, though, I saw his eyes were gentle and intelligent. I felt *he* wasn't swept away by the crowds, either, but expressed warmth and a simple joy that were catching.

And his words inspired me. They were as eloquent as I could have hoped for. He stood up for my values and demonstrated how they applied to the issues of the day. From that night on, I vowed to do my part to elect him.

Whenever he made appearances in the San Francisco Bay Area, the newspapers published his schedule. I went to as many rallies as I could. This involved enlisting the cooperation of my parents. When their energies ran out, I turned to a family friend, Dick Russell, a graduate student at Berkeley who had no interest in politics but who thought my youthful crush on "that old guy" was a hoot to watch. Once, at a rally, I was close enough to The Great Man to help him don his overcoat. He had bursitis in his right shoulder, he explained, from shaking all those hands. What a moment!

I threw myself into his campaign, licking stamps and stuffing envelopes by the thousands. When Eisenhower won, I was devastated but not discouraged. My preference for Stevenson was reinforced when Eisenhower never spoke out against the anti-Communist Republican Senator Joseph McCarthy and his hunt for "red agents" during the Army-McCarthy hearings.

When Stevenson won the nomination to run against Eisenhower again in 1956, I was right back at it, working as hard as I could, only to see him go down to defeat once more. I was heartbroken. I remembered that Stevenson had quoted Abraham Lincoln after his first defeat, "It hurts too much to laugh, but I'm too old to cry."

Four years later, when John Kennedy ran against Richard Nixon, I was involved once more, having been an early and enthusiastic reader of Kennedy's book, *Profiles in Courage*. But I never felt the overwhelming commitment I had pledged to Adlai Stevenson. Nor, I suppose, will I ever again.

By 1960 Eisenhower had proved to be, in my more mature eyes, not as bad a president as I'd expected. He was campaigning for his vice president, Richard Nixon, though. My opposition to Eisenhower was nothing compared to my dislike of Nixon, who, like Joe McCarthy, had been a "red-baiter" since his earliest Congressional campaigning days in California.

That year, my father, a member of the Commonwealth Club in San Francisco, was invited to a luncheon at which President Eisenhower was to speak. Wives and family members above a certain age could come, too. A political junkie, I was delighted to go, but not before I carefully removed my JFK campaign button from my coat lapel.

Our luncheon table at the club was close to the dais where President Eisenhower sat amid various local notables. So I made my plan. The moment the main course was over, while we waited for dessert, I approached the Secret Service man standing in front of Eisenhower and whispered in his ear. The man turned to the president, who smiled and motioned for me to approach. In those days a well-dressed young woman of eighteen could hardly be taken for a threat. After climbing the two steps fronting the dais, I looked down at the sitting Eisenhower, who smiled up at me expectantly.

I could have told him whatever was on my mind. I could have told him to his face that he was nuts to be supporting that arch-villain, Nixon. But when the moment came for me to speak truth to power, my manners got the better of me.

"May I have your autograph?" I asked, meekly.

"Why, surely," he replied, with his trademark broad grin and a wink of his eye. His charm was evident. He signed my outthrust program. When I returned to my seat, I saw he'd written his famous nickname, Ike.

My chief impression of the president was one I've never heard mentioned by any interviewer: As I stood over him, I noticed many little growths on his elderly bald head. They were red, green, tan, brown, and gray. Having for my entire lifetime seen photos of Eisenhower in black and white, I was struck by the fact he was in color.

It's your turn now

Further thoughts for readers, writers, and storytellers

Can you recall when you were first struck by events way beyond your home, school, family, and friendships? What happened to jolt you awake?

41: In the Front of the Bus

In 1987 I was getting adjusted to my empty nest. My daughter, Jessica, had just left for college. When I came home from work at night, the house seemed hollowed out. My core purpose, being a mother, had been snatched away, leaving only a blankness in its wake.

So when my husband, Stefan, suggested I join him on a trip to San Antonio, where he would attend a math conference—have I told you he is a mathematician?—the invitation was welcome. I had no idea I'd find the key to moving forward with my life.

San Antonio, with its River Walk and other tourist attractions, was no disappointment. I was having a great time when I happened to read that Rosa Parks, the famous seamstress-turned-civil-rights-activist, was coming to town for Martin Luther King Jr. Day. Rosa would lead a parade, the article said. She would ride in the front of a bus similar to the one she'd boarded in Montgomery, Alabama, in 1955, when she refused to ride in the back and thereby changed history.

The parade was to begin at a famous San Antonio hotel. Stefan and I decided to go there and glimpse Rosa before she entered the bus. Arriving early, we stood eagerly in a small crowd outside the rear entrance to her hotel, where the 1950s-era bus waited for her.

When she finally emerged, she was not triumphant, as I had somehow expected. She was solemn and overcast, clad in her own thoughts. Perhaps she was remembering Martin Luther King Jr., and what a loss his death was, especially for someone who'd worked with him early in the movement.

I caught her gaze and gave her my most exultant smile, but her face was shuttered. I thought of all the losses she had endured, and yet survived. My smile contained all my admiration for her simple stateliness, but it was to no avail. Mounting to her front window seat, she would not admit a shaft of sunlight into the gray day. She regarded us gravely as we stood beside the bus door. My gaze held hers, reflecting my delight at being with someone who had accomplished so much.

Then, suddenly, her shutters flew open and she smiled back—no small smile but a radiant one, filled with possibilities, ready once more for the road.

I have never forgotten that inspiring smile. It seemed to send a message: "Yes, life has its losses. They may seem to break you, but the question is, what do you do with the pieces? Stick to your essential truths, and life finds its path forward. You are the hero of your own story."

But wait a minute: didn't that mirror the message I had, unknowingly, sent to her?

I got what I needed from Rosa Parks that day. And perhaps, just perhaps, she got something she needed from me.

It's your turn now

Further thoughts for readers, writers, and storytellers

This encounter changed me because I was open to change. How have you determined your purpose in life as it has evolved through different phases?

42: East Meets West, and a Wall Comes Down

M y church has explored many issues confronting the world in the fifty years I've been a member. But at one moment world history came, embodied, to the doorstep of the Morristown (NJ) Unitarian Fellowship.

In 1989, during Gorbachev's *glasnost* era, the Cold War seemed to have been going on forever—certainly all of my sentient life. We took it for granted and didn't expect it would end anytime soon. Yet the thaw was coming and it would reach our small corner of the world.

Loosening Iron Curtain restrictions allowed a well-known Russian artist to visit the United States as part of a Soviet dissident poster art display in Madison, the town next door. There was one problem: he needed a sponsoring organization. Longtime Fellowship member Ludmilla Olsen, herself a Russian émigré, asked that the Fellowship sponsor Yuri Bokser's one-week visit. Since it cost us nothing, we readily agreed. He stayed at Ludmilla's home.

Yuri was a tall, slim, dynamic, chain-smoking young man whose natural skepticism about the world was balanced by an eager curiosity about America. That week we ferried him here and there, showing him how we lived—from ordinary people's homes to the mansion that served as George Washington's headquarters during two winters of the American Revolution.

When I took him to see a local supermarket, with its abundant supplies of fresh meat and vegetables, he did nothing to disguise his astonishment. Being with him renewed my own appreciation for our freedom.

A group of Fellowship members took him out to dinner and asked what he wanted to eat.

"Meat," he replied.

That one word told us so much about the reality in which he lived.

That very week, the wall between East and West Berlin was knocked down, the most dramatic signal to date that Soviet power was waning. We all gazed at our TV sets in amazement, watching this sudden global promise of expanding freedom.

Our minister, Rev. Paul Ratzlaff, wanted Yuri to participate in the service the following Sunday. He refused. At first he didn't explain why. Then he said he didn't think he could abstain from smoking for an entire hour. Finally, he gave in.

That Sunday morning Paul and Yuri talked about his life in the USSR, his visit, his impressions, and what the destruction of the Berlin Wall meant to him and to all of us.

As the religious education coordinator at the time, I helped the children separate into two groups. We constructed a wall of ignorance, fear, hatred, and suspicion (in the form of cardboard bricks) down the center of our sanctuary. Then the congregation cheered on the children as they gleefully demolished the wall and came together again. What a great moment.

When he got home, Yuri became creative director of a major advertising agency in Moscow. In 2002, sadly, he died. But I will always remember the whirlwind energy and enthusiasm he brought from the mysterious and crumbling Soviet sphere.

I can hear now what he said when we asked, "What was the most surprising thing you saw in America?"

"The airplanes," he said. "Not the military planes or jetliners we see at home, but the small aircraft that go darting about your sky."

When I see those small planes flying free, I think of Yuri and that hopeful moment in history.

It's your turn now

Further thoughts for readers, writers, and storytellers

Has there been a time in your life when you were touched, unexpectedly, by historical forces? Your grandchildren might like to read about it someday.

43: 9/14: The Aftermath

Three days after 9/11, as my husband and I headed to bed, I said, "I need to go there." He knew what I meant. The site of the World Trade Center was like the raw crater of a newly pulled tooth. The event, so far beyond our understanding, ached to be explored, to be understood.

So we found our way to the Jersey City waterfront—the closest we could get to the new reality.

A quiet midnight scene lay spread before us. At our feet, the Hudson River, shining with countless reflected lights, pushed its silent way toward the sea. Beyond it was the inimitable New York skyline, outlined against the rose-red nighttime backdrop familiar to city dwellers. The shoreline skyscrapers, like stout sentinels, hid the nakedness of the ruins but not the dreadful hole in the sky where the two towers had stood.

On the low horizon something had taken the place of the towers—a great furnace of light from the still-burning core. From this massive glow rose, at a 45-degree angle, white smoke that poured toward the foot of the island and into the darkness beyond.

At our vantage point it was so quiet, I could almost hear the great Earth turning on its axis. Bearing witness to the frantic search for survivors were small boats shuttling back and forth across the Hudson. They ferried weary rescue workers to respite on the Jersey side. The first responders were gray specters, smeared with ash and depleted from their hard work, as they emerged from the shuttle boats one by one.

They came from all over. The vans and pickup trucks in parking lots near the river bore license plates from Louisiana, Kansas, Wisconsin, and other states. Enormous trailers were parked there, too, as corporations, including Campbell's® Soup Company, dispensed sustenance to the workers.

While the first responders drank their coffee and soup, we shyly approached to thank them for doing the work we could not do. They answered us gratefully but briefly, saving their energies for the great work across the Hudson.

"It's good to feel useful," one man said.

As we walked among them, we spoke in hushed tones. Amid this monstrous disaster, everyone did.

Returning to the terrace by the river, we stood by some young people kneeling and keeping vigil over a clutch of glass-held votive lights of varying heights, like a small flickering city of hope threatened by erratic river winds. We stopped and relit a candle that had blown out, then another, then another. Soon rescuing that little city became our mission. There was wholeness there and a peace we hadn't felt for days.

Hours later we turned homeward, having filled our spirits with wordless meaning. We didn't know that on the far side of the continent, at the same time, my father rose from his bed and stumbled into the living room where an embolism, no doubt formed in the stress of 9/11, found its way to his brain and began the last chapter of his life.

It was a night woven of beauty and grief, of grandeur and loss. How could we distinguish them? They were one and the same.

It's your turn now

Further thoughts for readers, writers, and storytellers

September 11, 2001 was a day no one can forget. Have you written an account of where you were and how you responded to that world-changing time?

VIII: Traveling Lessons

44: O Little Town of Alamos

For me, one of the deep themes of the Christmas story is the power of being shut out, the power of welcoming, and the power of being welcomed.

Mary and Joseph, as the story goes, were turned away by the householders and innkeepers of Bethlehem. They found their welcome in a lowly stall where they made themselves at home and then welcomed the shepherds, angels, and wise men who sought them out.

At Christmastime in 1955, when I was fourteen, my own little family of three saw those themes of acceptance and rejection worked out in the timeless Mexican town of Alamos. We got there just in time for the final night of Las Posadas, an annual December ritual procession that recreates Mary and Joseph's entry into Bethlehem.

For three days, we had driven our 1952 Oldsmobile from the San Francisco Bay Area to the state of Sonora. As we turned off the coastal highway and crossed the final thirty-five miles of desert to Alamos, I wondered what we'd find there.

We knew the town had been a great silver mining center in the seventeenth century, when it was built. When the silver ran out in the eighteenth century, it became deserted. We also knew that the abandonment of this boom town had preserved its graceful architecture and that the Mexican government had made it into a national monument. At the time Alamos was occupied by Mexican families, American expatriates and tourists.

When we arrived we were immediately struck by its similarity to other ancient desert communities we had seen or read about. Imagine a place in the middle of nowhere so unspoiled that it has no gas station! Perhaps it wasn't so different from the place Jesus was born, only with automobiles as well as donkeys in the streets.

As we drove up to our hotel at dusk that Christmas Eve, a man named Antonio urgently greeted us.

"Vamanos! Vamanos! No waste time!" he said, in very broken English. "Las Posadas leaves now from the town square."

As we jumped out of our car, he handed each of us flickering candles. They lit our way through the darkening streets until we merged with a crowd led by the local Joseph and Mary and an angel, all illuminated by candlelight. We had read about Las Posadas, the ritual processions that reenacted Mary and Joseph's entry into Bethlehem. But now, travelers ourselves, we were in the midst of it.

Almost immediately, the crowd started moving through the colonnade-lined streets of the town, coming at last to a closed carved wooden door similar to many others we had passed. Deciphering the Spanish from a printed sheet, we sang out that we were poor people come from afar, needing shelter for the night for a woman about to give birth.

The answer came back to us from the other side of the door. Someone sang out, "This is not an inn, so keep going. We cannot open for you. You might be rogues!"

So we processed on through the darkened town until we stopped at another door. Again we sang, "Have mercy on us. God will reward you for it."

But a man inside sang back to us, "Go away now. If I get angry I will thrash you."

And so it went. At each door, our requests were mocked.

Finally, our procession came to a door where our pleas were heard. The voices from the other side of the door sang, "Enter, holy pilgrims, for though this dwelling is poor, I offer it with all my heart."

So Joseph, Mary, and the rest of us were welcomed into a large party with bountiful food, which we gladly ate as we shook off the desert chill and enjoyed the music of a mariachi band.

Hours later when we settled into our hotel, my mother remarked, "I think we just received the welcome of a lifetime."

We met many wonderful people that night, and friendships grew over our weeklong stay in town. That welcoming banquet yielded us invitations to a dance and a real Mexican wedding in the beautiful old church on the town plaza.

It was a magical time. The veil that usually parts tourists from residents was lifted. It was a week of deep encounters for all of us—some comic, some inspirational, and one, as you will see later, even tragic. That week of my life was a revelation in many ways.

The next morning, Christmas, my family abandoned our usual practice of bestowing gifts on one another and asked for directions to the poorest village in the area. There my parents and I passed out candies and coins to ragged children for whom December 25 was just another day. But as they examined their simple presents, we saw on their grimy faces the same wonder and delight we associated with children at home that time of year.

Later I got to know children nearer my own age in Alamos. Every day we played simple games together, teaching one another scraps of our different languages. The children were amazed to learn that my given name, Betsy, was not a saint's name, and explained to me they did not celebrate birth-days there. Instead, every child was celebrated on the day of the saint for whom they were named.

"Then you have no day to celebrate," they mourned, pitying me.

In the course of the week, we met amazing people, among them an American jailbird, a wise old woman, a bad-tempered cook who had murdered his wife but prepared our meals every day, and a little blond mestizo boy named Jesus, whose blissful smile I will never forget.

My mother kept in touch with the wise old woman for some years. She learned from her the comings and goings of the small town. The wise woman said there'd never been such a magical Christmas in Alamos as the one we experienced, and never again was it quite the same.

It's your turn now

Further thoughts for readers, writers, and storytellers

Can you recall a particularly powerful welcome in your own life? You may have been the welcomed one, or you may have been the welcomer. What made it so special?

45: Mr. Reese/Ross Was Let Out for Meals

In hindsight I see how my parents and I were so easily drawn into the conspiracy. The first morning after we arrived in the Mexican town of Alamos, my parents set their sights on exploring the old silver-mining community. We got in our car, whereupon Antonio, who'd greeted us at the hotel the night before, appeared at the curb.

"Can I help you?" he asked politely.

My mother, who'd studied Spanish in school, explained we wanted to see the town.

"Nothing simpler," said Antonio, motioning for my mother to scoot over so he could sit beside her. Seeing that my father was about to protest, he added hastily, "Afterward, you can pay me what you think is reasonable."

When this was translated, my father thought for a moment.

"Fair enough," he said.

Off we went. Antonio directed us to the top of a nearby hill.

"This place will give you the best view of Alamos," he said. We arrived at a dusty little plaza, shaded by a large old pepper tree. Nearby were ancient iron gates opening onto a walled courtyard.

The pungent scent of the pepper tree drifted over us as we peered down at the cream-colored, red-roofed town. Antonio said it appeared now much as it did two hundred years earlier when the silver mines were flourishing. We admired the ornate church that dominated the plaza in the town's center and the adobe buildings, fronted with handsome colonnades that protected the citizens from the beating desert sun.

We turned our attention to what lay behind the gates. On three sides of the courtyard was a timeworn building with small rooms opening onto the yard.

"What is this place?" my mother asked.

"Oh, this?" said Antonio. "This is the *juzgado*."

I pricked up my ears. Even a fourteen-year-old non-Spanish-speaker, having watched her share of Westerns, knew a *juzgado* was a jail.

A man approached the gates from the inside.

"This is the jailer," Antonio explained. Introductions were made. "Some of the inmates make things to sell. They earn a little money for themselves. Would you like to see?"

A bit reluctantly, my parents said yes. They probably figured they'd be obliged to buy junk. But they were pleased to discover well-made bolos— Western neckties made of thin, braided horsehair cording with slides of peanut stone, mounted on silver. After some negotiations, my father bought one. He put it on over his short-sleeved white shirt. The polished black stone, with inclusions of what looked like peanuts, showed off handsomely.

Then the jailer said, rather proudly, "We have an American staying with us. Would you like to meet him?"

Before anyone could muster an answer, we noticed that a tall, good-looking man with a ready smile was approaching the gates. Seeing we were in for it, anyway, my father agreed.

"This is Mr. Reese. He's staying here for a while."

We shook hands through the bars of the gate, feeling a little uncomfortable, but Mr. Reese was very much at his ease. He returned my father's somewhat restrained desert-greeting of "Howdy" with a full-press city-goer's "How do you do? A charming town, isn't it?"

We exchanged pleasantries about the local sights. Soon we were relaxed.

"You may see Mr. Reese in town sometimes. He eats his meals in the local restaurants," the jailer explained as my mother translated.

After that mysterious remark, my father decided it was time to move on to other sights.

That evening we ate dinner at a hacienda with a distinctly tropical air at the edge of town. Before dinner was served, guests were invited to lounge in hammocks. The restaurateur's tame macaw wandered among us, occasionally nipping one of us through the undersides of our hammocks.

Sure enough, just before we were summoned to the table, Mr. Reese, or Mr. Ross, as the hostess called him, appeared. He greeted us pleasantly, inquiring after our day. My parents were relieved when Mr. Ross, as he now seemed to be called, didn't insert himself at our table. He sat alone.

By this time my mother was beside herself with curiosity.

"We've *got* to learn more about Mr. Reese, or Ross, or Mr. Reese/Ross," she said.

"Eleanor, you must *not* ask that man questions," pronounced my father, who was somewhat given to pronouncements.

"Oh, no," she said. "I think I have a better way."

She smiled her secret, womanly smile.

Our hotel had rocking chairs out in front where guests could sit and relax in the shade of the colonnade. Right next door was the home of a woman we'd met at a party, Mrs. Harriet Preston, who also liked to sit in the rocking chairs. She struck up a lively conversation with my mother over margaritas.

Mrs. Preston was a retired American expat who'd made a charming home for herself in Alamos. As Mother and I soon discovered, she knew everything that went on in town and was happy to tell all.

"Oh, yes, I know about your Mr. Reese—or is it Mr. Ross?" she asked, settling in to tell a story.

"We call him Mr. Reese/Ross," Mother interjected.

"I like that one," Mrs. Preston answered with a connoisseur's relish. "It has the right touch of mystery."

I saw Mother and Mrs. Preston, with their mutual love of good gossip, were fast becoming friends.

"He came here about a month ago, hitching a ride into town, and was staying at one of the local hotels when a jeweler from Mexico City checked in, with his mistress," said Mrs. Preston.

From my fourteen-year-old point of view, this conversation was getting *really* interesting.

"It was not long before Mr. Reese/Ross had ensnared the aging jeweler in an all-night game of poker, meanwhile flirting with the mistress, who was, of course, young and beautiful."

"And as we know," said my mother, "Mr. Reese/Ross is a sandy-haired version of Rhett Butler."

"You've got the idea. So you will not be surprised to hear the jeweler's mistress connived with him in getting the jeweler to pass out, whereupon they robbed the poor fellow of $10,000 worth of jewels and high-tailed it out of town, heading for the U.S. border in the jeweler's car.

"Unfortunately for Mr. Reese/Ross and the mistress, the jeweler came to, almost immediately after they left. He sounded the alarm before they got very far. The two were apprehended before they had crossed the desert and reached the coast. They were brought back to Alamos and jailed."

"What became of the jeweler's mistress?"

"I think the solution to *that* problem involved a suitable exchange of money, and the recognition that you just did not put a lady in jail when the real fault lay with a man. The jeweler let the charges against her drop, presumably out of embarrassment."

"But as for Mr. Reese/Ross, of course they put him in jail," my mother said. "How does that explain letting him out for meals?"

"Mr. Reese/Ross is a real problem for the town. He is an anomaly: an American citizen with no money and no one, not even in the United States, to bail him out. How could there be justice for such a man?" Mrs. Preston said.

"Moreover, the custom in Mexico is for families to provide meals for prisoners. Mr. Reese/Ross has no family or even any friends to feed him. The solution they arrived at was for the jail to let him loose every noontime and dinner hour to eat at a local restaurant, which would be reimbursed for his food by the town."

"But how could they be sure that Mr. Reese/Ross would not simply skip town, given the opportunity?" Mother asked.

"Ah, remember, this is Alamos, an isolated desert town. In the first place, he had no transportation of his own, and he could not be expected to survive crossing the thirty-five miles of Sonoran desert to the coast highway on foot. Alamos is in the foothills of the Sierra Madre, and there is no other way out. So he would have to hitch a ride.

"Of course, everyone in town knows about him. And then everybody who comes to town is told about Mr. Reese/Ross, so they understand that they should not give him a ride."

Mrs. Preston smiled amusedly at us.

"After all," she said, "were you not taken to meet him on your first day here?"

It's your turn now

Further thoughts for readers, writers, and storytellers

Do you remember being kept out of grown-up secrets when you were young, and then finally being admitted to the strangeness of adult doings? What was that like?

46: Chui Is Short for Jesus

Chui, a shy thirteen-year-old boy with a radiant smile, was the waiter at our Alamos hotel that Christmas. A great favorite with everyone, he jumped to perform whatever small service we desired. My family got to know all the other guests at the eighteenth-century hotel because we all ate breakfast (and sometimes other meals) together at one large refectory table in the atrium garden.

You had only to look at Chui to guess his origins. His light-colored skin and dark blond hair almost told his story: he was the son of a Mexican woman who'd worked at a local hotel and an obviously blond American man who'd been passing through.

As Mrs. Preston told us, the woman, because she was unwed, had lost her job in disgrace. She was forced to go back to the rugged Sierra Madres from which she had come. Chui was her only child. Because she had become unwell, he was her only source of support. Chui sent money home out of every paycheck.

His story was known to all in this small place where everyone knew one another's business. In Alamos, gossip was a popular form of recreation. Before we left town, ten days after we arrived, we knew the life stories of just about everyone we met. At age fourteen, I learned quite a bit about life just by keeping my ears open.

Geraldo, the cook at our hotel, was a man in his late thirties, dark of complexion and expression. Unlike Chui, a social butterfly, Geraldo kept to himself and did not speak to guests. It was widely said he'd murdered his wife in Chihuahua and had fled here to Sonora, from which there was no extradition. The hotel owner knew of his unsavory past but didn't hold it against him because he was one of the best cooks in town.

To tell the truth, we guests were just a little afraid of Geraldo. We had to be reassured he had not *poisoned* his wife but garroted her. The thought of poison was too much even for the most intrepid among us.

Geraldo had formed a strong dislike of Chui, based as much as anything on the fact Chui received liberal tips at every meal, whereas Geraldo, who had cooked the delicious food we tourists so often praised, received nothing. Geraldo must have brooded about this circumstance for some time before he saw his opportunity—an opportunity that involved me.

Though a teenager who considered herself fairly grown up, I enjoyed playing with the Mexican children who hung out around the hotel, including Chui during his off-hours. My new playmate's real name, I was fascinated to learn, was Jesus. Chui was a nickname.

Back home, I'd had the same boyfriend for two years, so when thirteen-year-old Chui flirted with me, I did not take him seriously. I just enjoyed the playfulness of what, to me, was a charming diversion. Once, when Chui caught up with me by myself, he shyly kissed me—a butterfly kiss I returned. It did not occur to me that this was a very serious bond for Chui of the radiant smile.

Perhaps I should have known to think twice. I'd attended a holiday dance in the town with local citizens, U.S. expatriates, and tourists alike. During the festivities, two very different cultures came together, with results both delightful and unfortunate.

A young American tourist, the son of a dentist and perhaps seventeen, danced with the fifteen-year-old daughter of a townsman and enjoyed the experience. So he asked her to dance again. Neither could speak a word of the other's language, but their youth and high spirits carried them along. Then the young man asked for a third dance. What could have been more logical?

After that dance, the girl's father stepped forward and congratulated him: he was engaged to be married! Apparently in the local culture, three dances in a row indicated a proposal. The girl and her parents were horrified to learn this custom was unknown in the United States. A great deal of fence-mending was required.

Meanwhile, Geraldo had been biding his time. After Chui kissed me, Geraldo must have thought over the possibilities for our innocent relationship. He suddenly put aside his sullen manner and became friendly toward the fatherless Chui, who was surprised but glad to have the older man's attention.

A couple of days into this comradeship, Geraldo invited Chui to go for a beer. Chui gladly accepted his invitation. He was proud to stand up at the bar with his new friend. Geraldo further delighted him by showing off his new carved bone-handled knife, which he then placed on the bar between himself and Chui. After a few minutes' conversation, he teased Chui about me and then said something very uncomplimentary about me.

Ah, the power of *machismo*. Even this thirteen-year-old boy realized his honor had been challenged. He did just what he had to do, just what Geraldo expected him to do, before a room full of witnesses: he reached for that gleaming bone-handled knife and attacked Geraldo with it. The older man jumped back from the threat, giving time for all to see what had happened, before he disarmed Chui with practiced ease.

In no time word of the incident made its way back to the hotel. The owner could not run his hotel with such an animosity between two employees. He was faced with an unhappy choice: fire his cook, who everyone knew had deliberately set up the incident, or fire his waiter, who had, after all, grabbed the knife. It was easier to get a new waiter than to replace such a capable cook, so he fired Chui.

The hotel guests were up in arms. If Geraldo lost his job, they reasoned, he could always find another one, but by the rules of Chui's society, no hotel would take a chance on hiring the boy. He was ruined, as his mother had been before him. Chui would have to return to her home in the wilderness of the Sierra Madre. With no money to support them, how would they live?

The guests got together and signed a petition to the owner, insisting that Chui be given his job back. The hotel owner, faced with this open rebellion, agreed to rehire Chui. It was clear, though, that the arrangement would only hold until the last of the petitioners had left town. And that's just how it worked out.

So it was that the employers in Alamos turned their backs on Jesus, little Chui of the radiant smile. Would there ever be, for Chui, someone to open the door and welcome him in?

The night before we were to leave Alamos, I lay in my bed, staring up into the darkness of my high-ceilinged room. Something tragic had happened that I'd had no control over. Or did I? When I thought of that innocent kiss, and what had followed it, I felt the weight of the world's inequalities and the miseries that come from them. Something in me said, *Sometimes bad things happen and you have to admit to yourself you played a role in them, without being able to make things right again. The world is too harsh a place,* I thought, *to take any time off from being responsible.*

In acknowledging this to myself, I felt an unfamiliar sensation in my body, as if I were being stretched on a rack. In reality I was just growing up.

It's your turn now

Further thoughts for readers, writers, and storytellers

In the course of your life, have you ever made a serious mistake? And were you given the freedom to recover from it, or not? Either way, you might want to write about it.

47: Three Marvels by the Rio Grande

When I was eighteen, my parents and I visited the vast, remote stretch of Chihuahuan desert known as Big Bend National Park, in Texas. My cousin Phyllis and her family were stationed there. Her husband, Rod, a district ranger, knew the secrets of this ancient landscape, once occupied by Native Americans who left rock inscriptions for us to puzzle over.

My cousins lived at Boquillas, a ranger station directly across the Rio Grande from the Mexican town of the same name. Together, we explored the region by day. At night we sat on their deck overlooking the river and watched the star-filled night descend.

Phyllis and Rod entertained us with tales of their local adventures. Phyllis, a Spanish major in college, had a calling: she forded the shallow river in their pickup truck to deliver the babies of the impoverished, isolated Mexicans who were their nearest neighbors. After dinner, Phyllis played her guitar for us, singing familiar folk tunes and exotic Mexican songs.

One evening Rod said, "Tomorrow night Phyllis and I will take you out to see some of the outstanding features of our park. The moon will be full."

No matter how much we asked, he wouldn't say more.

"Wait and see," he said. "Wear your bathing suits underneath your clothes and bring these towels with you."

As it turned out, he introduced us to three marvels, all on the same unforgettable night.

The next evening, guided by the light of the moon, we drove upstream to the deserted ruins of what would have been called a motor court back in the 1930s.

"This used to be a spa, where people came to take the waters and heal from a variety of ailments," Rod said. He pointed toward the river's edge. "Over there is the mineral spring which flows out of the riverbank and is diverted into the foundations of the old spa building. Nothing remains of the spa except these stone foundations, which keep the waters full to overflowing. Just follow that path till you come to the hot spring. We can bathe there by moonlight."

And so we did, kept wondrously afloat by the mineral content of the water. Fortunately, the putrid sulfur smell of many a mineral spring was absent. As I lay back in the water, I looked up at the full moon. I took in the gentle water sounds of the river flowing beneath us. I became part of the pool, part of the moonlight, part of the flowing river.

Rod's voice seemed to come from far away.

"Long ago the Native Americans who lived nearby discovered the hot spring," he explained. "They built a small catchment basin so they could 'take the waters' and be relieved of many ailments."

"How long did it take to get results?"

I thought my mother asked that question because she had a "bad" shoulder.

"They believed you had to bathe there twenty-one times to get the full benefit," Rod said. "They transmitted this to the *Yanquis* who followed them and built the spa, which was abandoned in 1942. That's when the national park was created."

When we had bathed to everyone's satisfaction, we climbed out and dried off. As we dressed we shivered in the cold desert air.

"Now let's go and see the motel ruins," Rod said.

As we walked I wondered what could be of interest in the ruins of an old motel.

This building, constructed of stone like the spa, was more intact. There was a roof over it. Doors still blocked entry into every one of the six or eight rooms. One door was half-knocked off its hinges so Rod easily pulled it open. When he did, an enormous swarm of bats came rushing out. We instinctively put up our arms to protect our faces, but Rod reassured us.

"Don't worry about their running into you," he said. "They're great navigators and will easily dodge you."

He laughed at our dismay. We relaxed.

"They are guardians of the night sky," he explained. "They eat insects that bother humans."

I extended my arms toward the doorway as throngs of bats made their exit. *Thanks,* I thought, *and have a good night's hunting.* As they flew past me into the darkness, the flutter of a thousand wings stirred the air that touched my skin.

When the last bat left, Rod said he had one more surprise for us.

With that, he turned on his flashlight and shone it over the walls of the "bat cave." Ghostly images popped into the light—the desert in bloom, cowboys managing their herds, distant purple mountains. I could tell the scenes were once vivid but had moldered away during years of neglect. The images conjured Roman or Cretan murals, only parts of which have survived the ages.

"Where did these come from?" I asked.

"The story goes that sometime during the Depression an artist came through. He wanted to take the treatment but couldn't pay for it," Rod explained. "The spa owner made an agreement with him: he could stay if he would paint murals in the rooms. So all the rooms were decorated with sunsets, Indians, Mexicans gathered for market day, and other scenes of the period, vanishing now like the cowboys and Indians themselves."

Rod turned off the flashlight, leaving us in darkness. We imagined the hopes and dreams of all the people who had come and gone, and thought about the fleeting nature of all things. Beyond the door, we could dimly hear the Rio Grande as it flowed by.

Later, I found out that the murals were painted, not by a man, but by a "Mrs. Guy Lee, of Marathon, Texas." Only her husband's name remains to tell us who she was.

It's your turn now

Further thoughts for readers, writers, and storytellers

The national parks are a rich source of encounters, both with the natural world and the people who have gone before us. Write about one such encounter you've had. If you've always been a city person, why not stretch yourself and visit a national park?

48: Olympus in the Clouds

When I set off on a particular flight across the Atlantic, my fondest hope was for a little peace and quiet. I was a young mother traveling to England with my eleven-month-old daughter, Jessica, and my husband, Stefan. We took off late at night, well past Jessica's bedtime, so we and our fellow travelers endured the usual consequences—a very fussy baby. I held and comforted her as best I could, but I was no replacement for the crib we'd left behind.

Just after takeoff, though, the stewardesses rigged up a small crib/basket we had asked for that could hang from the bulkhead in front of us. At last we had a place to deposit Jessica. She could not have been more delighted. She understood immediately that this was her new sleeping place and knelt at the rim, beaming at the entire cabin even as the tears of a moment earlier still ran down her chubby cheeks.

I daresay the entire cabin beamed back at her with equal relief. She lay down, sucked her thumb, and drifted quietly to sleep. Having been granted the peace and quiet I longed for, we all settled in for the night.

I sat in a window seat. For some reason I did not close the window cover. Instead I stared into the total blankness of the night sky. After the ruckus of our takeoff, I wasn't as ready to sleep as my daughter and husband were. As I stared out into the darkness, I noticed a small flash of light from far below, just beyond my field of vision. Then I saw another and another.

They came from gigantic cumulonimbus cloud formations, peaking perhaps a thousand feet below us in the sky. Each time there was a flash, the cloud containing the lightning glowed brilliantly, illuminating the clouds around it with reflected light.

It was a rare sight: a gigantic thunderstorm over the north Atlantic, seen from above. We were flying at around thirty-five thousand feet. The towering thunderclouds below us were emblems of an enormous storm at sea. I imagined the sheets of rain down below, the overwhelming and relentless wind and waves, the roaring thunderclaps and searing bolts of lightning.

But from above the clouds, I saw a peaceful, magical world. As each flash faded, an afterimage of its cloud remained briefly stamped upon my retina. The stunning landscape's silent stillness and the smoothness of our passage heightened the dramatic effect.

It seemed we had come upon the Olympus of the Greek gods. We were witnessing their soundless communion, which we were permitted to observe but could not comprehend.

After that night, I often thought of that storm when faced with a toddler producing thunderous squalls. I mentally rose up a few thousand feet, making it easier to sail my aircraft in peace.

It's your turn now

Further thoughts for readers, writers, and storytellers

The early years of parenthood can teach much that applies to other life situations. Can you think of such revelations in your own life?

49: Down and Out in New York City

About once a year, my parents flew from California to New Jersey to visit their only grandchild—our daughter, Jessica—and, tangentially, with the parents of this precious being. One year, in February, they treated us all to the musical *Peter Pan*, starring Cathy Rigby. We enjoyed the show tremendously. Eleven-year-old Jessica was particularly thrilled when Peter flew over the audience.

We emerged from the theater to find an icy snowstorm was overwhelming New York City. Snowflakes swirled everywhere, greatly reducing visibility. Through snowdrifts and patches of ice, we made our way to our car and readied ourselves for the dark drive home, wishing we were flying through the tropics with Peter Pan.

Traffic was almost at a standstill. My husband, Stefan, inched us along until we came to an intersection with a traffic light. We had a good view of New Yorkers braving the elements as we chatted about the show.

I noticed an elderly man, poorly dressed for the weather and carrying a paper bag with a bottle in it. He'd obviously been drinking from it. He lurched his way across the street in front of us, but our thoughts were preoccupied with Jessica's delighted reaction to Cathy Rigby's performance.

A minute or so later, I glanced again at the intersection as we waited for the light to change. The old man was nowhere in sight. I saw the people who'd been crossing at the intersection alongside him. They had advanced about twenty-five feet. But where was that bum?

Given his condition and the weather, he might have fallen. Worse, he might have fallen in front of our car! Even as I inwardly called myself an alarmist, I stared intently past the hood of our car, just in case. *If I see anyone walking toward the spot with the intention of helping the old man up, I will signal Stefan to stop.* Time passed. People walked by. No one seemed concerned. I'd begun to relax when two things happened simultaneously: the light changed, and a small triangle of cloth appeared at the right edge of the hood, waving slightly.

I screamed for Stefan to stop. He did. People all over the intersection heard my scream, looked, and made their way to where the old man had fallen, directly in front of our bumper. They helped him up and guided him to the other side of the street. We proceeded, counting our blessings.

The oddest part of this encounter was that we soon found ourselves in the same position at the next traffic light. People crossed in front of us. By then we were fully alert to their movements. Our jaws dropped as another pedestrian fell directly in front of our car. He was surrounded with helpers immediately. The second man was well dressed. Is *that* what garnered him instant attention? Are New Yorkers, normally helpful in my experience, inured to the behavior of old drunks to the point they don't even see them?

If I moved to New York City, would I, too, become derelict-blind?

It's your turn now

Further thoughts for readers, writers, and storytellers

When you find yourself in the presence of a street person who may need help, how do you respond? How do others react? Is there a difference? Write about such a time.

50: The Man in the Wall

We'd been living for two weeks at the Quinta Saõ Gerónimo on the outskirts of Coimbra, an ancient city in Portugal, when I saw the man in the wall.

Until that moment in 1982, I'd cherished a certain fondness for the wall that surrounded the quinta. It sheltered our seventeenth-century villa and farm from the busy city of one hundred thousand people. Coming home from a long day at the university, where my husband taught under a Fulbright grant, seeing the wall told us we were nearly home.

There were plenty of walls in the city, of course, but none like ours. What made it unique was the coat of arms, shrouded in black cloth, which capped the entrance gate. The black cloth was a sign of mourning for the quinta's late owner, who, at the age of 102, had recently died from a fall down stairs—not at the quinta, we were told.

The family, a very old and distinguished one in Portugal, had many homes scattered around the country. Before the owner's death, the quinta had been empty for five years. Its ancient family chapel and monastery, fallen into ruins, had been subjected to the depredations of vandals. Housing is scarce in the ancient city. We were very grateful the old man's grandson, who had moved in after his death, allowed us to rent a part of his home for a month and share the services of his housekeeper, Alzira.

But I want to tell you about the man in the wall.

Halfway along one side of our wall, set into the stucco facing, was a small door. I never wondered much about it. I would have guessed a tool shed lay behind it. But why would a tool shed face onto the street instead of onto the olive groves behind the wall? I never asked myself that question until the day I saw the door ajar.

Inside, although it was very dark, was a man sitting up on a bed. He talked and gestured to another man, who seemed to be a visitor. The room couldn't have been more than four feet deep and ten feet long. There were no windows, of course. Something was wrong with the man on the bed. His arms and legs were contorted and moved unpredictably. He was very thin.

I hurried by, my eyes averted, embarrassed he might see my distress. That one glimpse was all I ever had. *A man lives in that wall*, I told myself, but I couldn't really believe it. I wanted to ask someone, but there was no one to ask. Alzira spoke no English. My Portuguese was rudimentary.

I might have asked our landlord. Although his English was good, he refused to communicate except through a translator—because of pride, a colleague had told us. The family was very old and very proud, and it would shame him to speak to us in English because he would be at a disadvantage. He might make a mistake.

How could I say to such a man, "I notice there is a man living in your wall"? For all we knew, anything we said or did might endanger the man's situation. No, it was impossible.

For a few days, the image of the man haunted me. Had I made a mistake? After all, I'd only had a brief glimpse. *Portugal is a poor country*, I thought, *but surely the government must provide, mustn't they?*

From that day on, the door remained firmly shut. We would only be in Portugal for one brief summer, and I was always being confronted with new things I only half understood. Eventually I did the usual thing: I put the man out of my mind—until two months later, on our last day in the ancient city.

By then we'd long since left the quinta and were staying in a former royal palace that the university owned. It was a royal palace in name only, since the king and queen for whom it was built never assumed the throne. They'd had to leave town suddenly when the dictator Salazar was overthrown.

But to us, the royal part was very real. As we were the only residents of the palace, we spread out a bit. My husband, Stefan, and I occupied the queen's suite, with its elegantly appointed reception rooms, while our daughter, Jessica, had a suite of her own down the hall.

We were told that all the furnishings were just as they had been when the "royal family" had lived there. When they left after the revolution a few years back, they took only the family paintings with them. I reveled in planting my feet on an Aubusson carpet in the morning when I climbed out of the queen's bed.

On our last day in the ancient university city, we decided to bring Alzira to see the palace. The quinta's housekeeper had lived in Brazil, South Africa, and Malawi. Once she had been rich, she said, with a big fancy house and four black servants, but then the men with the guns had come and taken it all away. She'd told us all about it, every day, with tears in her eyes.

As our Portuguese improved we came to understand more and more. She had to leave Africa, she told us, and come back to her native Portugal to earn her living as a housekeeper. Alzira was our first friend in that city. We wanted to share our newfound prosperity.

So we drove her to the palace, where she reclined delightedly on the queen's silk chaise longue, bounced up and down on the queen's bed, and asked the caretaker over and over in Portuguese, "Was this *really* a royal palace?" It was probably the first time she'd smiled since having all her teeth pulled two weeks earlier. With her new false teeth firmly in place, she insisted on having her picture taken in a dozen different poses around the palace, beaming fiercely for my camera.

As we took her home for the last time and drove through the gateway, I asked, "What is behind that door?"

"Oh, it is a man," she shrugged. "My boss lets him live there. Something is wrong with him." That's all she knew.

So there it was. What more was there to say? Alzira gave food to the stray dogs in the neighborhood, but the man in the wall was not her business. Perhaps the man in the wall was not our business either. But I can't forget him.

It's your turn now

Further thoughts for readers, writers, and storytellers

Have you come across extremes of wealth and poverty in your travels and been unable to make a difference? Writing about it will give you a chance to sort out your own reactions.

51: Coimbra Dogs

Dogs trotted through the streets of this large, ancient Portuguese city in 1982—large ones and small ones, scruffy strays, and well-tended purebreds. Independent, alone, they whiled away the daylight hours in Coimbra with friends in a downtown park or favorite alley.

They crossed streets near intersections, looking both ways, mostly, though some bore the marks of inattention, such as a broken leg, never set, dangling uselessly as its owner moved smoothly on the remaining three.

They weren't distracted by the errant smells that so tempt urban American canines, who go for outings only on leashes. These dogs were in charge of their own social calendars. At day's end they clearly knew where to go. Home was where they got fed and spent their nights.

Some owners were just plain oblivious to their dogs' condition, making it difficult to tell which were strays. One very large dog, an Irish wolfhound with a gray matted coat, may have fallen into this category. His rheumy eyes were so badly infected, I couldn't help but think his days were numbered. Yet day after day he made his way around town on arthritic joints. Somebody—a neighborhood butcher?—must have fed him, giving him just enough affection to keep his gigantic frame going one more day. My heart went out to him.

One day I caught sight of a small group of dogs hurrying somewhere. Something was up. Suddenly, an elegant Afghan hound bounded out of a side street. Pursued by a mélange of dogs, all hoping to win her favor, she was obviously the source of all the excitement. She was having none of it, however, and turned this way and that to avoid being caught. She raced down the street on her long legs, her beautiful coat flowing around her, her ardent suitors trailing behind. *She's safe from them*, I thought. *Not one was tall enough to reach such a rapidly moving target.*

I turned toward the University of Coimbra, where my husband was spending the summer teaching computer science.

The dogs passed out of my mind until I walked back to our neighborhood later. On an unpaved road close to home, I came upon the dogs, all sprawled in the dust, happily content but exhausted, as if they'd just seen a wonderful bodice-ripper of a movie. In the center of this mass of dog flesh, I spotted Old Rheumy, lying with his head on the Afghan's well-groomed coat. The two dogs were in a state of peaceful bliss.

The wolfhound may have been old and full of woes. He might not have been the handsomest fellow in town, but he was the tallest. And that's just what this occasion called for. This was his moment. He had seized it.

I guess it's true what they say—every dog has his day.

It's your turn now

Further thoughts for readers, writers, and storytellers

Dogs live among us, but have you ever noticed that they can have a culture all their own? Tell a story from your own experience.

52: In the Chinese Night, a Call for Help

During the seven summer weeks Stefan and I traveled around China in 1993, our most remarkable encounters with Chinese people came out of the blue—or in this case, out of the black of night, in the middle of nowhere.

About three o'clock in the morning, a small, excited crowd swarmed in front of our minibus, bringing us to an abrupt halt. "Us" meant five visitors from the West and our hosts, a half-dozen Chinese academics taking us to Huangshan, the famous sacred mountain range.

The trip so far had been arduous. We'd traveled all the previous day and were supposed to reach our destination at eight the previous evening. Our underpowered minibus, however, proved no match for the roadbed, which was very much under reconstruction. We didn't expect to reach the foot of the mountains till dawn. As we bumped and heaved through the night, we had poured a fair amount of energy into not complaining. Though no one was really sleeping, our group had been mostly silent for a couple of hours, each of us lost in our own thoughts, when suddenly the bus jolted to a stop.

We were still hours from the mountains, deep in a poor agricultural province not far from Shanghai, as our vehicle screeched to a stop. A group of excited villagers surrounded our vehicle, all shouting at once. Their huts were clustered at the side of the road.

"What is it?" we asked. "What do they want?"

"We don't know yet," our guide answered. "Perhaps they mean to rob us. Make sure your windows are rolled up."

I rolled up my window hastily. A discussion ensued.

Looking out, I saw a number of unarmed young Chinese men in their night shorts. They surely did not look like my idea of robbers. Even without knowing the language, I saw that the villagers were pleading earnestly for our help. Several young women, also very animated, joined them.

Some discussion took place in rapid Chinese. After a minute our hosts clearly pieced together a story. The matter seemed settled. Our guide rolled up the window and motioned for the driver to resume our trip. As we rolled along, he explained what had happened.

"They claim that the village's only bicycle was stolen, just now," he said. "They want us to catch the man for them, or at least give them a ride so they can catch up with him. He is just down the road, or so they said. But who can tell? They might be trying to trick us. I told them that we could not help them. They argued with me until I said that it was impossible because we had important foreign visitors in the bus. Then, of course, they understood and stepped aside."

Our minibus continued its lurching progress through the dark country-side. In a short while we overtook a lone bicyclist going the same way. Hunched over his handlebars, he pedaled like mad. No doubt he was the thief.

It seemed clear the villagers had told the truth. To make up for our unwillingness to apprehend the criminal, our guide hurled insults at him as we zipped by. We Westerners could not persuade him to turn back and let us grab the bicycle, or at least provide a little foreign aid to the stricken villagers.

"There is no time," he said.

Our group lapsed into its former silence.

The incident had ended, but I felt a deep pang. Here was a community of people so poor, they had only one vehicle among them—a bicycle, at that. How much it must have meant to them! If they noticed its disappearance so immediately in the middle of the night, how carefully they must have watched over it! What would they suffer without it? What would be the consequences of our refusal to help?

The next day we'd be hiking through stupendous mountain scenery, admiring giant peaks of vertical rock slabs as they rose from a drifting ocean of clouds. Our strange adventure would be half-forgotten. But the villagers would just be coming to terms with their predicament. *The story might have had a happy ending, I thought, if no one protected "important foreign visitors" from the upset of thwarting a crook.*

What must they think of us passing through their ancient landscape— we fortunate few absolved from responding to inconvenient requests? I thought of writing to the village and sending money for a new bicycle. But what was the name of the place? No one could say. It was just another poor settlement in the middle of nowhere—just one more group of people whose problems I could not solve or even comprehend.

It's your turn now

Further thoughts for readers, writers, and storytellers

When you were enmeshed in your own predicaments and someone asked you for help, how did you respond? And how would you respond now?

53: "Tell Me about Your Religion"

I n the middle of a sumptuous banquet luncheon in China in the summer of 1993, I unexpectedly became the focus of attention. Our host leaned across the large round table and addressed me directly.

"I believe you are talking about your religion," he said. He'd overheard me answer a question his wife had asked. "Please, I would like to hear what you are saying, too. Will you say it again?"

Professor Chang and his wife taught at the Hefei Institutes of Physical Sciences, where they were entertaining my husband, Stefan, and me, as well as several other Chinese and Western colleagues in a private dining room. Professor Chang, a vice president in charge of public affairs at the Institutes, had been questioning Stefan about how American universities fund their programs. He was, as his wife informed me *sotto voce*, "a very important man."

All dozen people at the table stopped their conversations to hear my answer to this important man's question.

I'd often found myself faced with this question, but seldom from someone who lived in such a profoundly different cultural context.

"We are Unitarian Universalists," I began. "As we see it, all human beings experience the great mystery of the passage of time and the inevitability of loss. We are all forced to choose how we will spend our time and energies, and we all have to adopt certain values by which to guide our decisions. We all have experiences of awe and wonder at a universe beyond our capacity to comprehend. Such experiences provoke in humans everywhere a religious response."

"China has several very ancient religions," Professor Chang said.

"Exactly," I responded. "As you can see right here in China, the religious responses of people around the world differ greatly. Faced with the same questions about the meaning of life and what comes afterward, people have constructed religions that provide very diverse answers. Not all of them can have the 'right' answers. And each is so sure of itself that they seldom learn from one another. We Unitarian Universalists think this is a great shame."

"But what can be done?" Dr. Chang shrugged. "People see things differently."

"UUs, as we call ourselves for short, do not all have to find the same answers to the unprovable questions. Instead, we share certain bedrock values—for example, a conviction that all human beings have inherent worth and should participate equally in determining their lives and beliefs. Because we recognize that all peoples face the same fundamental issues, we take great pleasure in learning the wisdom that has been expressed in cultures around the world—for example, many UUs study Buddhism, while still considering themselves Unitarian Universalists."

"You mean you may believe different things—about whether God exists, say—and you can even change your minds?" Professor Chang asked. He leaned over his plate and eyed me keenly.

"We recognize that defining our beliefs is a lifelong process, and that as our lives change, as our societies change, our personal answers may change, too," I said. "But whatever turns our lives take, we feel we need to remember that we are all part of the great human family and the Earth that sustains us. In a changing world we have a lot to learn from all our relatives."

I felt embarrassed to have made such a long speech though, to my surprise, people listened with great interest.

Professor Chang lowered his chopsticks, which had remained suspended above his plate while I spoke. He beamed at me delightedly.

"I think yours must be a very fine religion," he said. "I like your notion of a religion which learns from others and is open to change. It makes a lot of sense since, after all, the world *is* changing."

I thought of the changes Professor Chang had seen in his lifetime. Born after the end of the ancient Chinese empire, he would remember the Kuomintang, the coming of Communism, the growing worship of Mao Zedong, the hideous convulsions of the decade-long Cultural Revolution, the turning away from that intensity and, at that time, the coming of a capitalist economy within the framework of the old Communist political system. Through all these changes, he, and everyone else we'd met, had survived. The old certainties had passed away. I felt his openness to the future.

I tried to imagine the China of two decades from now—A China sharing a faith in democratic principles? A China dotted with Unitarian Universalist congregations? No, there my imagination failed me entirely.

I thought of Professor Chang's remark again when we arrived in Shanghai, the place Chairman Mao's Cultural Revolution had started, the city that had so wholeheartedly thrown itself into the barbaric actions of the Red Guards. No place in China had more wholeheartedly embraced the fervent doctrinaire Communism of that age.

But in 1993 Shanghai already was a far different place. Twenty years after the Red Guards, in this burgeoning modern cityscape, air-conditioned department stores lined the streets, their ample shelves overflowing with capitalist goods that people eagerly bought. Everyone in Shanghai wanted to cut a deal, wanted to go into business for himself, wanted to go into business with *you*.

To the Western mind, it is difficult to put together these different Chinas. How can the people have made such a vast change? Still, whatever the explanation, we could not escape the sense we were seeing the future of China. *Whatever happens next*, I thought, *the Chinese are ready for it*. I believed that, though they might make many mistakes, they would do well. After thousands of years of civilization and change, something essential remained, something enduring that is truly Chinese.

May China find its place in the world community, I thought, *and in turn share something of its ancient wisdom with us.*

It's your turn now

Further thoughts for readers, writers, and storytellers

Was there a time when you were challenged to sum up your belief system? What did you say then, and what would you say now? If you've never been challenged, challenge yourself.

54: Three Old Chinese Men Linger

When I travel, I come home with a mind laden with those I've met. They live there indefinitely, coming out, unsummoned, as required. Now, as old age encroaches, three ancient men appear to guide me onward.

The first was taking his caged canary for a walk in a Beijing park. Curious, I followed him and discovered a cluster of his cronies on benches, each with his own caged songbird. Gregarious old men and birds all chatted and chirped away, weaving a tapestry of togetherness that seemed to give them purpose—even joy.

The second was a sunbaked gardener at a Buddhist temple in Xi'an, raking waves into its smooth-pebbled, leaf-strewn garden. The many worshippers at the shrine were clearly new to religious ways, after the recent lifting of Chairman Mao's long ban on religious observances. You could see from their body language that they were not connected with the deeper meanings of Buddhism, and were basically just begging favors from the Buddha, whose large gilded wooden statue presided over the shrine.

In contrast, the elderly gardener, with his serene half-smile, was mindfully instilling meaning into every pass of his rake. His religion was apparent in every motion of his body.

The third was a shrunken old man in a village far to the west. Clad only in a ragged loincloth, he squatted on raisin-dry haunches beside the road in a prosperous village of truck-gardens, turning the crank on his popcorn-popper, a small wire cage perched above a glowing bed of charcoal. Something about him drew me in. Perhaps it was his air of composure in the face of a hard fate, which had brought him to this lowly station.

He refused to let me take his picture—out of pride, I suppose. I had no way to tell him I wanted to photograph him in admiration of his dignity, not to sneer.

Foiled, I bought a paper bag of peppered popcorn and carried him away in my head.

They were just three old men, but each one taught me, wordlessly, something about how to be old.

It's your turn now

Further thoughts for readers, writers, and storytellers

You met them for a moment but remember them forever. Who were these strangers, and what do they mean to you? In the writing, you may learn.

55: Reflections on a Lotus Pond

I sat beside a lotus pond, in the shade of a classic Chinese carved wooden pavilion, brightly painted in traditional shades of red, green, and gold. I'd arrived by way of stepping-stones that curved across the water. I was there to watch. Nearby, three boys practiced on the only skateboard I had seen in the China of 1993.

The place was part of Tsinghua University in Beijing, where we were staying in the guesthouse. Once, though, it had been part of the extensive grounds of the old imperial summer palace, brutally destroyed in 1860 by allied European nations during the Opium Wars.

It was late morning. The lotus flowers had opened their graceful pink-tipped white petals in the golden sunshine. The lotus roots, I had learned, rest in the pond muck below. What I saw were the flowers and leaves rising in two tiers—the first round, flat leaf, or pad, floats on the surface of the water while the stalk continued to ascend. It bore a second leaf about a foot higher that shaded the first, and then a luminous lotus blossom, that rose above both.

As I watched, I noticed the water that had collected in the small hollow at the center of the higher leaf. It was bubbling, as if at full boil, though it never boiled away. Like all lotus ponds, this one struck me as mysterious, full of impenetrable secrets.

Only after I returned to America did I learn a secret of the lotus plant: it is one of three plants in the world known to generate its own heat, like mammals and birds. Perhaps my subconscious awareness of that heat corresponded to how I felt in the presence of a fellow being. But for that moment, I just let the mystery be.

Observing more closely, I noticed the small jungle world created between the high and low leaves—a secret world unto itself, humid and quiescent, inhabited primarily by small insects. Among the rounded lotus pads at water level, duckweed filled in the entire pond's surface area, making the water, just a millimeter below and essential to this small ecosystem, completely invisible.

Just then, through my green lotus jungle, a small bird came hopping. It was similar to the sparrows I'd seen in the countryside following the rice harvest, or sometimes, alas, heaped on a banquet platter. She hopped across the surface of the water from lotus pad to lotus pad, appearing quite at home as she successfully pursued a breakfast of insects.

Little sister, I said to her in my head, *you are not a water bird with waterproof feathers. One misstep and the water will swallow you up. What makes you so confident that you will not fall in and drown?*

An answer came back to me as I watched: *O woman, are you so confident of what moves beneath the surface of your fortunate existence? I know what I know, which is that this is a fine morning for bugs.*

On she went, hopping sure-footedly among the lotus pads.

While I watched intently, a little girl of about nine approached me, followed my gaze, and asked, in perfect English, "What are you looking at?"

I explained to her about the lotus-jungle and the little sparrow who hunted insects there. She shook her head and frowned.

"I've been looking at this lotus pond for years," she said, "and I never saw what you are showing me."

"You are very young," I told her. "Practice looking closely at the world and, bit by bit, you will see many new and amazing things all your life."

She lingered a while longer before going off to watch the skateboarding boys. I thought of the generations of emperors and their silken retinues who had once delighted in sitting beside such lotus ponds. I thought of the cataclysms, military and political, and the ultimate cataclysm of relentless time that brought an end to their lotus world. And I knew my sparrow sister, my nine-year-old companion, and I were embarked on the same perilous passage.

I got up to go, crossing the flat stones that dotted the pond, and thought, *It is, indeed, a fine morning for bugs.*

It's your turn now

Further thoughts for readers, writers, and storytellers

This important message was given to me by one of China's innumerable sparrows. The sparrow and I, the Emperor and I, are You and I, I and Thou, diverse and yet One. You can learn that from anything, if you look closely enough. Write about a time you learned something from a surprising source.

Notes and Acknowledgments

This book is a work of non-fiction: it all happened to me, and I tell it to the best of my recollection. At the same time, I am changing the names of some of my early-childhood friends, to protect their privacy. The same is true of some locations, in my Berkeley neighborhood and some wilderness areas whose whereabouts are not mine to divulge.

I owe a great debt of gratitude to the many people who helped me with this book, especially my small family, Stefan and Jessica Burr, and my first and most encouraging reader, Carol Titus, as well as Jay Anthony and Laura Nass, Judi Marcy, Janine Torsiello, and Jim Blanton; informants David Schooley, Rod Broyles and his daughters, Elizabeth Rivera and Bea Bachenburg; readers Mary Olmsted, Susan Niculescu and The Madison Group of Women Who Write; and more readers among Cedar Crest residents: Rose Marie Armstrong, Maxine Colm, Julia Craven, Inge Goldstein, Debbie Greenberg-Zeigler, Ruth Karr, David Lewis and Carolyn Burr, Frank Melchior, Virginia Mollenkott, Pat Thaler, Jim Gallagher, and Ann Whitestone; and consultants Lorraine and Bill Ash, Beth Smith, and Judith Lindbergh.

About the Author

Born in San Francisco and raised in the stimulating world of Berkeley, Betsy Burr's California childhood was rich in storytelling. She was an only child in a three-generation home, her dinner table festooned with her grandmother's tales of times past, which were annoying to Betsy's mother but made vivid by a keen ear for dialog and rich sense of humor. Betsy also loved her sequestered bedtime hour with her mother. It yielded nightly insight into the private lives of friends and neighbors, whether dramatic or amusing— accounts that fascinated a child who wanted to understand what made people tick.

Her education at Pomona College, UC Berkeley, and Cornell University led to an MA in English Literature and helped her make friends of the great storytellers from Geoffrey Chaucer to Jane Austen to Dylan Thomas.

Later, living in New Jersey with her mathematician husband, Stefan, and their daughter, Jessica, Betsy held a variety of jobs. As a state legislative analyst, she unraveled complex issues for New Jersey state senators. Later, she was the head of religious education at her church.

For over 40 years she taught hundreds of people from her own congregation and around the country to tell their own stories in a Sunday morning context. She also founded and directed Earth Camp, a summer day-camp where she especially loved weaving for eager children true tales of interconnectedness to teach them about their home planet. Later, she ran a business selling hand-made Chinese teapots, recounting for customers the classic tales behind the imagery that adorned them. All the while she was crisscrossing the country regularly to look after her invalid mother.

At the heart of her life-story has been meeting a wonderful diversity of people and other creatures, some of whose stories she tells here.

She co-authored a denominational pamphlet on how to create lay worship services, wrote seven musical comedies and plays for her church, and published a libretto for a commissioned oratorio, "Legacies," and a chapbook of poems, "At Play in the Field of Horses." This is her first full-length book.

She now lives with her husband Stefan in a large New Jersey retirement community where storytelling abounds.

Made in the USA
Monee, IL
23 May 2020

31710265R00154